SPECIAL EDUCATION IN TIBET

This book analyses the value orientation system of education in Tibet and examines the special education interventions aimed at children with disabilities in the region. The authors draw on their interviews with students, parents and teachers to shed light on how education is viewed by the general population in Tibet.

The book looks at themes such as traditional Tibetan education, the ways in which value orientation affects the development of disabled children, the role of special education interventions in building self-esteem and confidence and the importance of developing pedagogical care and special schools in Tibet. It also reviews China's existing legal provisions and policies dedicated to persons with disabilities in comparison with Tibet. Finally, it emphasizes the role of practicing social acceptance for children with special educational needs and recommends developing special education interventions based on the cultural foundation and real social conditions of the ethnic group.

Based on in-depth qualitative and quantitative research, this book will be of interest to teachers, students and researchers of education, special education, curriculum studies, sociology, anthropology, disability studies, minority studies and cultural studies. It will also be useful for educationalists, special education institutions, policymakers, social activists and NGOs.

Miloň Potměšil is Professor of special pedagogy. He holds a PhD degree in psychology and a PhD degree in special pedagogy. His research interests include deaf studies, educational psychology, behavioural management and deafness and psychology of special support to parents of impaired children. He is also an active participant in international research projects and gives lectures in foreign universities. Since 2014, he has been Professor Emeritus at Faculty of Education, Sichuan Normal University, and Researcher at Research Centre for Multicultural Education, Sichuan, China. His recent publications include *Inclusive Education of Learners with Disability: The Theory vs. Reality* (2020). He has also published articles in various international scientific journals.

BuQiong holds a PhD degree in Special Education and is Lecturer at the Faculty of Education, Sichuan Normal University, China. His research is mainly focused on ethnic special education theory and practice and ethnic education. He has presided over several projects, including "Value Orientation of Special Education in Tibetan Areas", among others. He is involved in compiling the Sichuan Normal University's school-level textbook, *Microteaching Training Course for Special Education Major*, and has published more than 10 academic papers including "An Overview of Special Education Development in Tibetan Areas" and "Dignity Education and the Cultivation of Dignified People", in the *Journal of Northwest University for Nationalities*, *E-PEDAGOGIUM* and other domestic and international journals. In addition, he has compiled, edited and translated the textbook *Physical Teaching of Normal Schools*, participated in the compilation of the textbook *Microteaching Training Textbook* and published two co-authored monographs including *Walking in Gubao Mountain Village: Story of Cultural Construction and Educational Practice*.

SPECIAL EDUCATION IN TIBET

Perspectives on the Education of Children with Special Educational Needs

Miloň Potměšil and BuQiong

Routledge
Taylor & Francis Group
LONDON AND NEW YORK

First published 2022
by Routledge
2 Park Square, Milton Park, Abingdon, Oxon OX14 4RN

and by Routledge
605 Third Avenue, New York, NY 10158

Routledge is an imprint of the Taylor & Francis Group, an informa business

British Library Cataloguing-in-Publication Data
A catalogue record for this book is available from the British Library

Library of Congress Cataloging-in-Publication Data
Names: Potměšil, Miloň, 1955– author. | BuQiong, author.
Title: Special education in Tibet : perspectives on the education of children with special educational needs / Miloň Potmešil and BuQiong.
Description: Abingdon, Oxon ; New York, NY : Taylor & Francis Group, 2022. | Includes bibliographical references and index.
Identifiers: LCCN 2021045447 (print) | LCCN 2021045448 (ebook) | ISBN 9780367644055 (hardback) | ISBN 9781032213941 (paperback) | ISBN 9781003268208 (ebook)
Subjects: LCSH: Special education—China—Tibet. | Children with disabilities—Education—China—Tibet. | Inclusive education—China—Tibet.
Classification: LCC LC3987.C67 P68 2022 (print) | LCC LC3987.C67 (ebook) | DDC 371.90951/5—dc23/eng/20211012
LC record available at https://lccn.loc.gov/2021045447
LC ebook record available at https://lccn.loc.gov/2021045448

ISBN: 978-0-367-64405-5 (hbk)
ISBN: 978-1-032-21394-1 (pbk)
ISBN: 978-1-003-26820-8 (ebk)

DOI: 10.4324/9781003268208

Typeset in Sabon
by Apex CoVantage, LLC

This publication is an outcome from the US-WEINOE 1S-1213-001-1-10-06 research project and the research project of Research center of multicultural research Sichuan Normal University in Chengdu, PRC.

CONTENTS

TABLES

1

INTRODUCTION

Education in Tibet

The Tibetan nationality is one of the 55 minorities in China. Some live on the Qinghai-Tibet Plateau, the Roof of the World, which is also a land of snow because of the snow-covered mountains all around. There are three ecological zones, including a rural area, pasturing area and farming-pastoral region, with their own respective ways of production and working. Tibetan people have their own language, along with the traditional culture and religion of Tibetan Buddhism. From birth to death, most Tibetan people lead a farming life or a shepherd's life. Simple production and labour skills are all learnt in practice. People think that the purpose of schools is to educate children to pass examinations, find an office job and escape from a farmer's or shepherd's life limited by the seasons or weather. They do not understand that a school education can bring changes to production and life in farming and stockbreeding areas, or they do not know the values and significance of school education for human survival and development. With such an understanding of school education, it is generally considered unnecessary to enable disabled children to go to school. Especially before 2000, there were almost no schools for children with special needs.[1] Disabled young people could not go to general schools and failed to obtain a school education. Since 2000, some special education schools have successively been established in the Tibetan areas to meet the educational needs of the minority of impaired children.

In other words, schools in the Tibetan areas have developed rapidly since the establishment of the Chinese government. An undeniable fact about education in the Tibetan areas is that the education system aims to cultivate state cadres and it creates the need for a hierarchy in education rather than fulfilling students' needs for survival and a happy life. Such simplicity in its purpose and utilitarianism in its value orientation have led to certain negative impacts on the construction of education and culture in the Tibetan areas. It is critical to explore whether such issues exist in the initiation and development of contemporary special education in the Tibetan regions and what the impacts are. On the basis of past research findings, when it comes to children with impairment, the majority of Tibetan people focus on the

 DOI: 10.4324/9781003268208-1

children's future lives and the purpose and value of education. The value is mainly shaped by the purpose of how to create a happy life for children.

If we assume that the value orientation of education with a focus on children's future happy lives and perceptions about education are better adapted to the basic theories of special education interventions, we can conduct an in-depth analysis of the interventions of the development of special education through addressing the following questions: What is the relationship between such a kind of value orientation of education and the traditional value orientation of the Tibetan region? What is the relationship between such a kind of value orientation of education and the value orientation of traditional Tibetan education? The next question is what the value orientation of education in the Tibetan areas should be? How will it affect the educational development of disabled adolescent Tibetans? In this interventional process, based on the types of conditions and objectives, how do special schools, local communities and families conduct their interventions? On the basis of answering these questions, this research tries to understand the special education interventions aimed at adolescents with a disability in Tibet. In other words, this study intends to analyse the value orientation of education in the Tibetan regions with detailed survey data on cultural knowledge and the actual social situation. The survey is designed to gain an understanding of the attitudes of Tibetan students, parents and teachers towards education. The study also discusses interventions in the special education of adolescents with disabilities on the basis of the value orientation of education.

The special education interventions in the Tibetan areas

In China, Tibetan people are mainly distributed in the regions of the Tibet Autonomous Region (TAR) and Qinghai, Gansu, Sichuan and Yunnan provinces (as shown in Figure 1.1), with a total population of about 6.4 million people. The TAR is the main Tibetan region and is central to Tibetan cultural, political and economic development. The Tibetan regions in Sichuan Province are the central areas of Kangba in the traditional regional division of Tibetans. They include two Tibetan autonomous prefectures and one Tibetan autonomous county, which constitute the second most populous Tibetan settlements outside the TAR. Therefore, some basic data were collected in these two settlements. The results show that only four of the five special education schools founded in the TAR since 2000 have enrolled students. There are a total of 656 students and 173 teachers in these schools. The Tibetan regions in Sichuan Province have four existing special schools with more than 260 students and about 70 teachers.[2] The TAR has a total of 32,000 disabled young people who are under the age of 15.[3] Ganzi Prefecture has a total of 1,889 registered disabled young people, which does not include those disabled

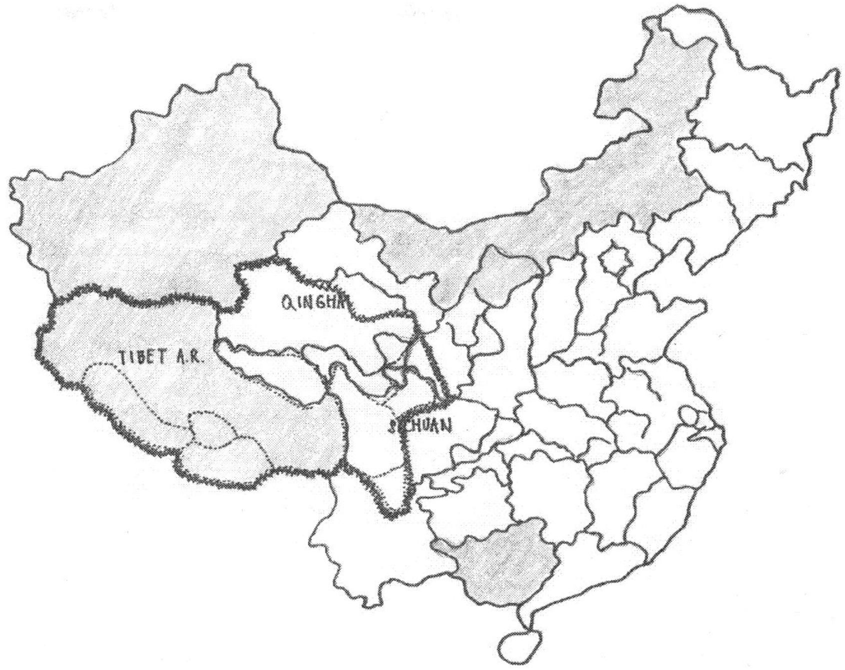

Figure 1.1 Map of the People's Republic of China[6]

young people who are not officially registered.[4] Special education in the Tibetan regions of other provinces, such as Qinghai, Gansu and Yunnan, even lags far behind these two places. Only four schools enrol students and maintain regular teaching in the Tibetan regions of those provinces. The total number of students in those schools is not less than 300.[5] In the Tibetan regions, the development of special education is extremely lacking in terms of equipment, organizational capacity, special personnel and community services. Therefore, it can be stated that the current development of special education interventions in the Tibetan regions actually focuses on the development of special schools themselves, rather than the improvement of the special education system. On the basis of our previous survey and findings, this is the key issue challenging the development of special education in the Tibetan regions. Therefore, in order to promote more sustainable and adaptive development of the special education system to the needs of disabled adolescent Tibetans, it is critical to conduct more in-depth and comprehensive research studies to address the aforementioned questions.

Tibetan area as an interesting space for research

The relative backwardness of special education in the Tibetan areas, as well as the extreme shortage of local researchers, has been mentioned repeatedly earlier. Having a sense of social responsibility alone may not lead to an effective research result. We also need great enthusiasm and an interest in the field. One of the researchers, Dr. BuQuiong, grew up in the Tibetan areas of Sichuan Province, and has engaged with minority education research and work for nearly 20 years. There are limited research studies being conducted in the field of the development of minority education in China, and the existing studies have somewhat biased and subjective findings. In this era of advocating the people-oriented development of education, very limited attention is paid to the development of the special education system and disabled people in the Tibetan regions. Therefore, it is essential to conduct a more in-depth study in this area.

Education as an interesting topic

What can be explored?

We will explore the aims of education of the older, middle-aged and young population in agricultural, pastoral, semi-pastoral and township areas in Tibet, as well as the education of impaired adolescents and its context, in order to find out how these age groups perceive their education. On the basis of these findings, we will systematize the value orientation in different areas in Tibetan age groups, historically and in terms of practicability, as well as the value orientation of education of adolescents with disabilities. Further, we will focus on school education and locate the needs.

Also, we will examine the origin of value orientation and its alternative purpose of special education for children in the Tibetan areas through a cultural perspective in order to explore the theoretical, methodological and practical implementation strategies for the development of Tibetan special education.

Additionally, we will systematize the alternative purpose of school education by comparing the value orientation of special education and general school education in Tibetan areas.

Finally, we will explore the complex methods and strategies of special education interventions aimed at adolescents with disabilities on the basis of the value orientation of Tibetan special education.

The way to get answers

(1) Through a discussion of value orientations in Tibetan special education, we will synthesize existing perspectives on special education and

summarize the theoretical and methodological perspectives that can be used to explain the development of special education in Tibetan regions in order to attract people to conduct further research on the promotion and development of special education in Tibetan regions.

(2) We will seek a rational value orientation for school education in the Tibetan areas and provide theoretical references for the purpose of school education and curricula for general and special education schools in Tibet.

(3) The society of the Tibetan areas has a unique status in the current civilization. The empirical studies of value orientations in the development of Tibetan special education provide theoretical perspectives and methodologies for a multicultural type of school education through value orientation studies of special education for children in Tibetan areas.

Going into deep details

After getting a research idea, perhaps from making observations of the world around us, the next step in the research process involves translating that idea into an answerable question (Marczyk, DeMatteo, & Festinger, 2005, p. 7), such as: What is the quality of special education interventions aimed at adolescents with a disability from the perspective of the value orientation in Tibet? The following questions lead to deep details about the topic:

(1) What are the value and value orientation of Tibetan traditional culture?
(2) What is the popular value orientation of education like in the Tibetan areas at present?
(3) By what kinds of value orientation of education are today's Tibetan special education schools affected?
(4) What kinds of cultural knowledge and life skills are needed for adolescents with a disability in the Tibetan areas?
(5) What should the special education interventions aimed at adolescents with a disability in the Tibetan areas be?
(6) How is school education enlightened by value-based special education interventions for adolescents with a disability in the Tibetan areas?
(7) Who or what influences the attitudes of secondary school students to education?
(8) What is the relationship between the respondents' age and their relationship to education and whether this relationship changes with age?
(9) Whether gender has an impact on education?
(10) Whether the type of school attended has an impact on the relationship to education?
(11) Whether the relationship to education is influenced by parental education?

Seven important relations to be described

1 The value orientation of education in the Tibetan areas has a close correlation with the value orientation of Tibetan traditional culture.
2 The value orientation of education in the Tibetan areas is not significantly different for all areas and age groups.
3 The special education interventions aimed at adolescents with a disability in Tibet have a close correlation with the special needs of adolescents with a disability.
4 There is no relation between the factors and the age of the respondents.
5 There is no relation between the individual factors and gender.
6 There is no relation between the factors and the type of school attended.
7 There is no relation between the factors and the education of the parents of the respondents.

Concept of related key terms

Value: The definition of value varies in different scholarly works. In this research, value refers to certain content in

> the relationship between the subject and object. The content is whether the object meets the needs of the subject and whether it is consistent with the subject and serves the subject. An affirmative answer, namely what we call 'good', signifies a positive value; the negative answer is what we call 'bad', that is, a negative value.
> (Li, 2004, p. 30)

"It is about the dynamic development arising from continuous evolution of the utilitarian relationship between the subject's needs and the object's attributes" (Ruan, 2004, p. 46). On the basis of the aforementioned understanding, the definition of value in this research is that the object meets and is approximate to or consistent with a need of the subject. In terms of this definition, it may be observed that "need" is especially important, and "need" decides value.

Value orientation: A value preference that evolves into a significant belief after a long period of time can be called a value orientation. It is substantially the choice or selection of, and pursuit or yearning for, certain values of the object based on the judgement of such values by the subject.

Value orientation of education: The value orientation of education means the intention or tendency of the subject while making value setting and value expectation against the educational object according to the educational needs of its own survival and development in the case of taking education as some social object. Such value setting and value expectation are a kind of value choice, i.e. selecting a certain scheme or several ones among the several value relationships between educational value as the subject and education as the object, so as to meet the subject's educational needs to a certain extent (Wang, 2002, p. 33). In short, the value orientation of education is the selection or choice of, and pursuit or yearning for, educational value; it is targeted at the future.

Adolescents with a disability: In this research, "Adolescents with a disability" mainly refers to adolescents aged 13–18 who have hearing, visual and mental disabilities.

Special education interventions: A special education intervention refers to the diagnosis, treatment, education and training of children with special needs. In this research, it can be interpreted as the treatment, education and training specific to the aforementioned needs of disabled adolescents, aiming to help them develop their capabilities, so as to let them become independent, adaptable and dignified in society. In China, the common models of special education interventions include special schools, integrated education in general schools (learning in a regular class), special education resource centres, rehabilitation centres for disabled children, family rehabilitation, community rehabilitation, etc. However, this research involves special education interventions aimed at adolescents with a disability in the Tibetan areas, where models of special education other than special schools have not been created yet.

Notes

1 In 1997, a blind German woman subsidized the establishment of the Lhasa Blind Children's School, the first special school in Tibet. Because of various restrictions, the author has not been able to enter this school for investigation.
2 Data source: the survey conducted by the author.
3 Data source: Tibet Autonomous Region Disabled Persons' Federation, 1987 Investigation data.
4 Data source: Ganzi Disabled Persons' Federation.
5 Data source: the survey conducted by the author.
6 Provided by the Author.

2

SPECIAL PEDAGOGY AND SPECIAL EDUCATIONAL INTERVENTION

Initial information

Although Tibet has a long history of treating disabled young people and family intervention therapy, in most cases, those treatment systems are informal traditional physical therapy and family treatment, mainly for the purpose of adaptation to a livelihood. In addition, there are no research studies explaining the use of traditional therapy for treating disabled young people. Tibetans only have a short history of the school-oriented development of special education, which means that the standards and formality of special education interventions provided to disabled young Tibetans have become a crucial programme. Given the special geographical location, socio-cultural background and biophysical conditions of the Tibetan regions, the consideration of local socio-cultural values in the development of special education is crucial. To this end, a more systematic literature review of national and international studies on the development of special education will be conducted to find more appropriate research perspectives and methodologies for the research design.

This research mainly discusses value orientation-based special education interventions aimed at disabled young people in the Tibetan areas. It is the study of the theory and practice of the "special education interventions" that are most deserving of being expounded and referenced for research experience and methods. Being somewhat broad conceptually, the term "special education intervention" is rarely seen in special education-related studies. A widely used term that has a similar meaning is "early childhood intervention", which mainly concerns the issues of intervention from birth to preschool, or from birth to primary school and even to secondary school. The age at which a specific intervention is provided varies between countries and social and cultural environments. Special education in the Tibetan regions is also closely associated with the current development of special education in the country and bigger regions. The lagging behind of special education in the Tibetan regions has already been frequently discussed. This study, based on the past and present development of special education as well as

DOI: 10.4324/9781003268208-2

the future developmental trend of special education in the Tibetan areas, defines the target of special education interventions as disabled teenagers (with special needs) aged 13–18. Therefore, in this review of international and mainland China's special education interventions, the development of early childhood interventions is primarily discussed and illustrated. Additionally, the review of Tibetan special education interventions will comprehensively describe the development of special education and the progress of research on special education in the Tibetan areas.

The research data used to describe special education interventions in mainland China, as well as the development and status of special education in the Tibetan areas, are derived from tools such as China National Knowledge Infrastructure (CNKI) and Google Scholar; foreign research refers to the relevant research literature in English. As English-language literature pertaining to Tibetan special education has not yet been found, the literature related to special education interventions in a broad sense in this research is mainly gained via querying and collection from ERIC, Google Scholar, E-Book of Palacky University Library, etc.

Early childhood intervention as a way of support recognized worldwide

An early childhood intervention is a support and educational system for very young children (aged up to 6 years) who have been victims of, or who are at high risk of, child abuse and/or neglect. Some states and regions have chosen to focus these services on children with developmental disabilities or delays, but Early Childhood Interventions are not limited to children with these disabilities (Wikipedia On-line Dictionary, 2017). Early interventions are beneficial to compensate for the shortcomings of children with special needs as early as possible, so that they can grow, both physically and mentally, as normally as possible, thus improving their social adaptability (Yan, 2003). This section begins with a brief review of the stages of the development of foreign special education, followed by a discussion about the development of early childhood interventions abroad.

Developmental stages of special education intervention

There have always been exceptional learners, but there have not always been special educational services to address their needs (see Holmes, 2004; Metzler, 2006). It is generally believed that the development of special education can be divided into three stages (Qian, 2008). Special education can be defined as educational and social services provided by preschools (Vargas-Barón, Janson, & Mufel, 2009, p. 8), schools and other educational organizations to children, usually between the ages of 2.5 or 3 years and 18–21 years. The first is the stage of diagnosis and treatment dominated by the medical model, focusing on disability and obstruction. The second stage is dominated by the psychological model, focusing on testing and classification. The third is the social model-dominant stage. According to Deng Meng (2001), the development models of U.S. special education have gone from scratch, from isolated boarding education back to the mainstream and to inclusive education under vigorous development. Lipsky and Gartner (1998) analysed services for the disabled at different historical stages on the basis of key issues, including who the service object is, where to provide services, what the process is and who provides services and what the goal is. They classified the development of special education into three stages from another perspective, namely the era of institutionalization, the era of deinstitutionalization and the era of community members. In the era of institutionalization, children with special needs or the disabled mainly received daily care from adults in unified and isolated institutions. In the era of deinstitutionalization, children with special needs and disabled people returned to the family, special classes and workshops for learning and living, and appropriate services may have been selected from the service selection system according to their degree of disability. Differently from the previous two historical eras, in the era of community members, everyone is treated equally, as are other intact individuals; children with special needs and disabled people return to the family, ordinary classes and community agencies to learn and live, while parents and educators are committed to cultivating them into qualified community citizens. The differences in the classification from the various stages of the development of special education actually reflect the same theme, i.e. evolution from discrimination against and exclusion of disabled people to the advocacy of human rights and equality and to recognition of differences and promotion of fair understanding and acceptance.

Development of early childhood interventions

Proposed in the United States in the 1960s, the term "early childhood interventions" mainly refers to the use of remedial measures to compensate children receiving their education in an adverse environment. Once proposed, this concept of compensatory education triggered extensive attention globally and directly led to the birth and implementation of a series of intervention programmes and methods in the United States and the rest of the world, so that early interventions were promoted and developed around the world. The U.S. 94–142 "Individuals with Disabilities Education Act (IDEA)", in particular, specifies that children with special needs and young people aged 3–21 receive free public school education, and the compulsory education for children with special needs is advanced from school age to preschool age. In 1986, an amendment to this Act provided for the provision of individualized family service plans for disabled infants. Japan and other countries implemented early interventions aimed at children with special needs in forms such as establishing special classes in ordinary kindergartens (Wang, 2000).

Early interventions are a support and education service system that includes at least intervention technology, parental involvement and social support and education services. Deng Meng and Yan Tingrui (2016) stated that when it comes to the technological development of Western special education interventions, with the human research of disability pathology and the development of science and technologies of detection and treatment, compensatory education for disabled individuals has gradually improved. In recent decades, researchers of special education have conducted multidisciplinary exploration and research on the operative technologies, including behavioural interventions and rehabilitation training of children with disabilities. For example, early researchers developed the technology of "behavioural correction" based on behaviourism. The technology of behavioural correction suggests that the behavioural disorders of children are mostly negative. It focuses on changing the children's behaviour by controlling the consequences and tends to adopt "punishment" as a single behavioural intervention model and strategy (Bambara & Knoster, 2009). After the 1980s, the application of behaviourism in special education began to shift from the traditional "behavioural correction" technology to "positive behaviour support". Positive behaviour support is a more comprehensive approach to replace punishment for children with special needs with behavioural problems in a positive and instructional way, featuring the method of systematic change to rebuild the individual living environment. In recent years, the response to intervention (RTI) has become a new intervention model coping with student diversity by schools and classes. Under this model, the adjustment and reform of teaching and intervention are conducted on the basis of an intervention response, and methods proved to be effective are adopted for teaching on the basis of dynamic assessment of students (Fairbanks, Sugai, Guardino, & Lathrop, 2007).

Social support and parental involvement in early childhood interventions have been initiated and popularized in Western education in recent decades and are guaranteed by legislation dealing with special education in many countries. Parental intervention refers to the rights and obligations of parents to participate in the education and growth of their children, including both family education and participation in school management and education (Qiu & Wang, 2010). Researchers generally believe that all successful interventions for children with disabilities necessitate parental involvement. The early intervention providers should focus on, but not be limited to, formal intervention institutions in society; what is more important is to mobilize families, neighbours, churches, etc., who are the preferred support and with whom it is easier to strengthen the functioning of the family.

In 1994, the World Conference on Special Needs Education clearly put forward the idea of inclusive education and discussed various aspects of its implementation, including curriculum provision, classroom organization, evaluation system, teacher training, special education centres, community service, parental involvement, the role of non-governmental organizations and early education for disabled children (Zan, 2016, p. 26). The *Framework for Action on Special Needs Education* and *Salamanca Statement* have had a significant impact on early interventions aimed at children with special needs in inclusive education worldwide. The British government published a series of influential documentary policies such as the *Warnock Report* and the *Green Paper on Special Education* and has clearly proposed that special education should be dominated by inclusive education and great importance should be attached to parental involvement and early interventions. In the United States, *the Head Start Plan* (1998), *Individuals with Disabilities Education Act* (1997) and *No Child Left Behind Act* (2001) effectively guarantee the smooth implementation of early intervention programmes, including a differential diagnosis for each child with special needs and an individualized family service plan and educational plan. Potměšil and Valenta (2006) elaborated on the diagnosis of children with special needs by means of interviews, questionnaires, school products analysis, testing and other methods and tools, highlighting the importance of joint diagnosis and treatment by specialists, social workers, doctors, psychologists, etc.

In conclusion, foreign special education and its research are developing rapidly, and the research on early childhood interventions is rather fruitful. Moreover, the development of inclusive education makes it possible for each student with special needs to obtain an effective intervention (Růžičková, 2017). But research on special education interventions aimed at children and teenagers after preschool education is rarely found in the literature.

The previous description briefly shows the development and research status of early childhood interventions in foreign countries and also introduces several developmental stages of foreign special education. Foreign studies directly related to this research are effectively impossible to find.

Development of early interventions on the Chinese mainland

Early childhood interventions represent an important field in special education. Therefore, they represent an integral part of special education research. On the Chinese mainland,[1] there is abundant literature on research findings in the field. The following sections consist of three parts – a definition of early childhood interventions and legal provisions concerning them, theories about early childhood interventions in existing research results and the practice of early interventions aimed at children with special needs.

Definition and legal basis

In the existing literature, different scholars on the Chinese mainland give different definitions of an early intervention. They include:

> An early intervention is a special educational and training tool used to increase the intelligence (or ability) of infants who deviate or may deviate from their normal growth and help them acquire certain living abilities and skills.
>
> (Mao, 1990, p. 215)

> In the special education field, [early intervention] mainly refers to therapy and education services provided for preschool children. It helps the children in their full social, emotional, physical, and cognitive development, enabling them to enter the normal education system or accept as little special education as possible.
>
> (Piao, 1996)

> Early intervention is a generic term for organized, targeted programmes covering prevention, identification, treatment and education, and training for children under the age of 5–6 who deviate or may deviate from their normal growth.
>
> (Wang, 2000)

> Early intervention is a series of stimulation and training activities for infants.
>
> (Huang, Li, Su, & Yang, 2000)

> In a broad sense, early intervention refers to a series of measures of prevention, identification, treatment, and education for preschool children who have or may have developmental disabilities, helping these children grow healthily and normally.
>
> (Lei, 2008)

Among the aforementioned definitions, some include early diagnosis, early treatment and early education for disabled children, while some exclude early diagnosis and only place the emphasis on treatment and education. In addition, these definitions show different targets of early interventions. Some cover children who have or may have developmental disabilities and exclude gifted infants. Some cover all children, while some cover children who deviate or may deviate from their normal growth, including gifted infants. It can be seen from the existing literature that the targets of early interventions in China are currently limited to children with special needs

(Yang, 2003). Therefore, the connotation and a target definition of an early childhood intervention need to be further standardized and unified.

Special education is an integral part of the education system of any modern civilized nation, and early interventions aimed at children with special needs are an important part of a nation's special education system (Zhang, 2016). The term "early childhood intervention" is not explicitly used in China's existing legal provisions and policies on persons with disabilities, but early intervention is closely associated with early education and early diagnosis. Therefore, considering the legislation on early childhood interventions, we first learn about legal provisions concerning early education and early diagnosis, including *The Law of the People's Republic of China on the Protection of Disabled Persons* (1990), *the Regulations on the Education of Persons with Disabilities* (1994), *the Maternal and Infant Health Law of the People's Republic of China* (2008), *the Opinions on Further Promoting the Reform and Development of Special Education during the Tenth Five-Year Plan* (2001) and *the Regulations on Disability Prevention and Rehabilitation* (2017). Second, a small number of studies related to the construction of laws can be found in the documents. For example, Zhang Lingyan (2016) pointed out the importance of early education for children with special needs and the necessity of the construction of a legal system. In brief, the construction and research of the legal system related to special education have garnered more attention, but research on implementation and the effect of existing legal provisions is lacking.

Theories about early childhood interventions in existing research results

On the basis of an analysis of the feasibility and necessity of early interventions, Wang Yan (2000) stated that there are two kinds of theories about early interventions. One is the biological theoretical basis of early interventions. The other is the psychological theoretical basis of early interventions, regarding specific training methods for early interventions in the case of children with intellectual disabilities. This theory is based on the operant conditioning proposed by B. F. Skinner, which was originally used for animals and then applied to children's education in connection with promoting family interventions aimed at infants. An important theory that affects early intervention is ecological system theory. According to the theory, infants are most dependent on their parents, and their living environment is mainly the family system, so early interventions aimed at infants can be implemented at home.

It can be seen from the aforementioned theoretical studies and other documents that China's research on interventions aimed at children with special needs is very weak. A detailed study on research activities focussed on early intervention in Mainland China was presented by Ling and Potměšil

(2017). Most of the research papers did not clarify their theoretical bases but focused on introducing specific practices and the operation of early interventions, and the research did not go beyond the theoretical framework mentioned earlier. Therefore, indigenous theoretical studies need to be strengthened.

How early childhood intervention works

In addition to the aforementioned studies on definitions and legal provisions, as well as theories about early childhood interventions, another important field is research on the practice of early childhood interventions. Documents on research on practice are much more numerous than in the previous two fields. Research on practice can be divided into two aspects. The first is the introduction of analysis and methods of the implementation of an early childhood intervention, such as: *The Effect of Early Intervention on Toddler Development* by Huang et al. (2000); the American Special Education Intervention Model by Jia (2011); Discussion of Early Interventions Aimed at Children with Special Needs by Yao Dan (2012); Application of Sandplay in Interventions Aimed at Children with Special Needs by Li Fangfang and Yang Liu (2015); Thoughts on Parents' Participation in Early Interventions Aimed at Children with Special Needs by Chen Xiumin (2013); Teachers' perception of the RTI implementation feasibility in Chinese inclusive early childhood education (Zhang, Liu & Yixin Lin, 2019); Ecological System Model and Revelation of Early Childhood Interventions in European Countries by Chen Jing (2008); An Investigation on the Current Situations of Community Interventions Aimed at People with Disabilities in Shanghai by Zhang, Jiang et al. (2007); Decision making in auditory interventions aimed at children with special needs by Liu, Zhang et al. (2008); Decision making in language interventions aimed at children with special needs by Huang, Zhang et al. (2008); An Investigation on the Needs of Families and Developmental Support of 71 Autistic Children by Huang, Zhang et al. (2009); Early Interventions Aimed at Autistic Children – A Three-Way Training System by Zhou and You (2007); Autistic Infants Joint Attention: Development Models and Early Interventions by Wang, Jia et al. (2016); The Autistic Child: Behavioural Intervention in Rehabilitation Status and Suggestions by Liu Hui (2010); On the Deficits in Facial Expression Recognition in Children with ASD and Clinical Interventions by Liu, Mo et al. (2014); Case Study on Early Interventions Aimed at Mentally Handicapped Children – Understanding Graphics and Hand-Eye Coordination Training by Xu (1995); Discussion of Model Construction of Personalized Comprehensive Interventions Aimed at Children with ADHD by Liu Yanju (2013); Means of Coping with Hearing-impaired Children in Families and Family-centred Early Interventions by Liu Shenlin (2010); A Case Study on an Early Intervention Aimed at a Child with a Hearing Impairment by Li and Zhang

(2007) and Conditions and Countermeasures of Rehabilitation of Deaf Children in China by Sun (2004). These studies introduced many special education intervention methods from abroad, but the indigenization of the studies on the basis of social and cultural differences is not enough. There are many studies on interventions aimed at autistic children, but studies on the practice of special education interventions aimed at children with other types of disabilities are still lacking.

In general, studies on early childhood interventions have taken shape, but there are no expert teams that integrate resources for collaborative research. There are also few indigenous studies on intervention theories and practice methods. Research on turning early intervention operation skills into early education programmes is not sufficient. In-depth research on parent-participated and community-supported intervention modes is needed.

Special education in the Tibetan areas

Special education in the Tibetan areas started at the turn of the century. It was marked by the establishment of special education schools. The conditions were not ripe for early assessment and diagnosis, intervention and prevention and treatment for children with special needs. At present, almost all the knowledge and related research on special education are being developed along with the development of special education schools. Therefore, the following contents will be discussed from two aspects – the development of special education in the Tibetan areas and the development of special education research.

Development of special education in the Tibetan areas

Before 2000, "special education" was an unfamiliar concept for most people in the Tibetan areas and there was not one special education school in any of the Tibetan areas. Middle- and low-grade physically disabled and mentally disabled children could study in general schools, but the schools failed to meet their special learning needs, so they could only adapt to the learning environment and conditions in the same way as general students did. In early childhood, blind, deaf and seriously mentally disabled children might have received medical treatment and rehabilitation training. If the effect of the training was not good, rehabilitation training could only be done at home on the family's own initiative and there were no conditions for the children to go to school. Just because of the lack of understanding of special education, neither a systematic and normative special education diagnosis nor early interventions took place in the Tibetan areas. Therefore, the development of special education lagged far behind that in the mainland and other minority regions.

Legal frame for special education in the Tibetan areas

From the perspective of the global trend of the development of special education and of human rights, the implementation of special education through the national policy and legislation has become an important part of the education policy of different countries, and it is a basic scale to measure whether the special education requirements of the disabled of a country are met, whether the opportunities to participate are equal and whether equal human rights are enjoyed. The national policy has also become an important driving force for the development of special education. Although China is behind the Western developed countries in terms of its special education legislation, the issue of the education of the disabled has been covered many times in the relevant laws and regulations since the founding of the People's Republic of China in 1949. To be specific, subject to Article 45, the *Constitution of the People's Republic of China*, "the State and the society provide assistance in the arrangement of the labour, living, and education of the blind, the deaf, the mute, and other disabled citizens". This was the first time that special education for the disabled was stipulated in a fundamental law of the State. *Several Opinions on the Development of Special Education* is a policy document for the development of special education in China which covers three spheres: guidelines and policy, goals and tasks and leadership and management. The *Law of the People's Republic of China on the Protection of Disabled Persons* (1990) was the first special law protecting the rights of the disabled of China. There are nine articles in Chapter 3 "Education", and the following provisions are laid down: the State protects the right of the disabled to receive education equally; the people's governments at all levels should regard the education of the disabled as a part of the cause of national education, carry out uniform planning, enhance the leadership and create the conditions for the disabled to receive education; the government, society and school should take effective measures to solve the practical difficulties faced by disabled children and juveniles in their schooling and help them go through compulsory education; the people's governments at all levels should provide textbooks free of charge to disabled students and students from the needy families of the disabled who receive compulsory education and provide the bed and board and other expense subsidies. For disabled students and students from the needy families of the disabled who receive other education beyond compulsory education, subsidies should be given according to the relevant national regulations. Pursuant to Article 12, the *Education Reform and Development Programme of China* (1993),

> the education of the disabled should be stressed and supported. The governments at all levels should regard the education of the disabled as a part of education and develop the education of the

> disabled by separately setting up schools for the disabled, general schools recruiting the disabled, and the like.

The *Regulations on Education for the Disabled* (1994) are an administrative law of the State Council for the education of the disabled, for the purpose of protecting the right of the disabled to receive education and developing the cause of the education of the disabled. In accordance with Article 10, the *Education Law of the People's Republic of China* (1995), "the State supports and develops the education of the disabled". According to Article 38, "the State, society, school and other educational institutions should implement education based on the physical and mental characteristics and requirements of the disabled and provide assistance and convenience to them". Subject to Article 5, the *Action Plan for Vitalization of Education Facing the 21st Century* (1999), "close attention is paid to special education, great efforts are exerted to provide opportunities for the vast majority of disabled children and juveniles to receive education, and their autonomous and self-improving spirit and survival and development abilities are cultivated". Subject to the *Law of the People's Republic of China on Compulsory Education* (2006),

> the people's government at the county level or above should set up an appropriate school (class) which implements special education as required, so as to implement compulsory education for the children and juveniles of the right age with a visual disability, hearing and speech disability, or mental disability. The special education school (class) should be provided with places and facilities corresponding to the study, rehabilitation, and living needs of disabled children and juveniles. The general school should admit disabled children and juveniles of the right age who have the ability to receive their general education through learning in a regular class, and provide assistance in their study and rehabilitation.

The *Plan for the Construction of Special Education Schools in the Central and Western Regions of China* is a document of the Ministry of Education and the National Development and Reform Commission for the construction of special education hardware. Its overall goals are as follows: the central and local governments make a joint investment in the construction of about 1,150 special education schools in the central and western regions, and an independently established comprehensive (a combined organizational system school of two or more kinds among three kinds of schools for the blind, the deaf and the mute, and the mentally disabled) or a single special education school for a prefecture-level city and a county with a population of more than 300,000, which has basically been achieved; the conditions for running a school of the existing special education school type have obviously been improved. Subject to the *Opinions of the State Council and the Central Committee of the Communist Party of China on Promoting the Development of the Disabled*, developing education for the disabled is regarded as the primary task in promoting the development of the disabled in an all-round manner. Additionally, the document stresses "developing the preschool rehabilitation education of disabled children, accelerating the development of special education in the senior high school stage, and encouraging and supporting the general institutions of higher education to open a special education major. Gradually settling the issue of the education of the seriously physically disabled, the seriously mentally disabled, the blind, the deaf, children and juveniles with cerebral palsy, and autistic children and juveniles" are mentioned. Chapter 10 of the *Mid- and Long-term Education Reform and Development Programme of China* specially discusses special education, and there are three clauses:

(1) Care and support for special education. Special education is a basic approach to promote the comprehensive development of the disabled and help the disabled integrate better into society. The governments at all levels should accelerate the development of special education, bring the topic of special education into the local economic and social development plan and list it on the agenda. The whole society should care about and support special education. The comprehensive abilities of disabled students should be improved. Close attention should be paid to the potential development and compensation for defects, and the awareness of disabled students to face life positively and integrate comprehensively into society and their self-esteem, self-confidence, self-reliance and spirit of self-improvement are cultivated. The vocational skill and employability upbringing of the disabled students is enhanced.
(2) Improve the special education system. Having regard to the government's plan, by 2020, there will be a special education school in every city (prefecture-level) and county (city) with a population of more than 300,000 and many disabled children and juveniles. The schools at all levels should positively create conditions to admit the disabled and constantly expand the learning in regular classes and the special education classes of general schools. The level of the popularization of compulsory education of disabled children and juveniles is comprehensively improved, the development of education in the senior high school stage for the disabled is accelerated, the vocational education of the disabled is robustly carried forward and close attention is paid to the development of the higher education of the disabled. Preschool education for disabled children is developed according to the local conditions.
(3) Perfect the special education guarantee mechanism. The State establishes the basic standards for running a special education school, and the local government establishes the per capita public fund standard of

> the students. The investment in special education is enhanced. General schools that admit disabled students are encouraged and supported in creating the study and living conditions for disabled students. The team building of special education teachers is strengthened, and relevant measures are taken to implement the treatment of special education teachers. In the commendation of excellent teachers, the proportion of special education teachers is increased. The subsidy to disabled students from families with financial difficulties is enhanced. Free education at the senior high school stage for disabled students is gradually implemented. A batch of major projects, including the development of special education, are implemented. A batch of special education schools are reconstructed, expanded or newly constructed so that there is a special education school in every city (prefecture-level) and county (city) with a population of more than 300,000 and many disabled children and juveniles; the necessary teaching, living and rehabilitation training facilities are added and the conditions for running a school are improved for the existing special education schools; professional training is implemented for special education teachers to improve their level of education and teaching.

The *Special Education Promotion Plan* is a national action plan jointly formulated by the Ministry of Education, the National Development and Reform Commission, the Ministry of Civil Affairs, the Ministry of Finance, the Ministry of Human Resources and Social Security, the National Health and Family Planning Commission and the China Disabled Persons' Federation. The full text is divided into four parts. The overall goals are as follows: inclusive education is comprehensively advanced so that every child can receive suitable education. A special education system characterized by a reasonable layout, the connection of study phases, the connection of general schools and vocational schools and a combination of medical rehabilitation and educational training is preliminarily established, and the conditions for running schools and educational quality are further promoted. The special education service guarantee mechanism characterized by public finance in the dominant position, social support, complete coverage and smoothness and convenience is established and improved, and the guaranteed capacity of special education is enhanced. The special education work pattern featuring government-led departmental cooperation and the participation of all parties is basically formed, and the promotion capacity of special education is strengthened. Three tasks are put forward. First, the level of popularization is improved. In particular, for those disabled children and juveniles who do not enter a school, individual arrangements are made for them to receive compulsory education. Second, the guaranteed conditions are enhanced. The normal running of special education schools is guaranteed, and the level of the running of schools is improved. Third, the quality of education and teaching is promoted, and optimal special school courses and teaching material systems are established.

The promulgation and implementation of these policies and laws and regulations have boosted the significant development of special education in mainland China. Remarkable results have been achieved in such aspects as the promotion of the degree of cognition of people for disabled students, improvement of the right of access to education of disabled students and the attainment of the achievements of disabled students. However, in terms of the actualities of the Tibetan regions, for a long time, these legal provisions did not leave obvious effects on the development of the education of the disabled in the Tibetan regions. Besides, according to a practical survey, the development of special education in the Tibetan regions is far behind that in mainland China and it is far from matching the specific development goals required by the aforementioned legal provisions.

As an autonomous region whose main residents are Tibetans, Tibet has not promulgated any legal provision for the development of special education. Sichuan, Qinghai, Gansu and Yunnan Provinces, which have Tibetan autonomous prefectures, only mention the development of special education in the regions inhabited by minority nationalities incidentally on necessary occasions, and there are almost no specific regulatory and policy documents concerning the development of special education in the regions inhabited by minority nationalities. The officials of some relevant competent departments of these provinces and autonomous regions have rather limited knowledge of special education. In recent years, as the phrase "everyone enjoys the opportunity to receive education fairly" has become increasingly popular, a balanced development of education has been comprehensively implemented, and specific and explicit requirements for the development of special education have been raised in the *Mid- and Long-term Education Reform and Development Program of China* and the *Special Education Promotion Plan*. The development of special education in the Tibetan regions is being accelerated, and relevant research on special education in the Tibetan regions is being facilitated.

Conditions for the disabled people in the Tibetan areas

In any society, any nation, or any historical period, people with disabilities are discriminated against and excluded. Being religious, all Tibetan people have a very commendable tolerance and can fully respect and accept disabled children, while the disabled also have a good ability for self-recognition and social adaptation. Through long-term observation, it can be seen that disabled people will not be greatly discriminated against in Tibetan society. Of course, different types of disabilities have different social adaptations.

The physically disabled: The disabled have normal language competence, so they can adapt to social communication, but different conditions may occur when they adapt to intact people's production and labour according to different types of physical disabilities and degrees of disability. They will generally acquire life skills appropriate to themselves according to their actual conditions. For instance, a person with a lower limb disability can learn how to sew by hand.

The deaf: Due to the loss of language competence, the deaf can only communicate with others with self-created gestures, creating certain barriers when they communicate with intact people. As they have four limbs and their visual sense is normal, they can adapt completely to intact people's living style. They can take part in any productive labour that can be done by intact people.

The blind: Without loss of language competence, the blind can normally communicate with intact people. But without visual perception, they cannot be occupied in production and labour like intact people and they even have certain difficulties with independence in life.

The mentally disabled: The middle- and low-grade mentally disabled can communicate with others smoothly, and they can also adapt to production and labour which requires only limited strength. The seriously mentally disabled cannot communicate with others normally or participate in the production and labour intact people work on, and they also have poor social adaptation.

From the previous descriptions, various people with disabilities adapt themselves well to social communication and exchange. They all have a certain degree of difficulty in doing productive labour except the deaf (including those with a hearing impairment), but they can always find something they can do. It should be noted that the types of disabilities mentioned here are well known in the Tibetan areas and most persuasive in defining the disabled. A more detailed classification of disability has not yet been formed or become familiar in the Tibetan areas. Also, from the descriptions mentioned earlier, it can be concluded that there were neither a rehabilitation organization and community service for special education nor any special education schools before 2000, so the disabled had almost no chance to go to school. However, they were clearly recognized and helped by family members and others in the village with respect to their social and life adaption.

The current situation of the development of special education in Tibet

Since 2000, with the proposal of, and general attention to, educational equality and balanced development, education and special education in the regions inhabited by ethnic groups have had unprecedented development opportunities. The Ministry of Education of the Government of China issued the "Special Education School Construction Plan in the Central and Western Regions during the 11th Five-year Plan (2006–2010)", "National

Medium and Long-term Education Reform and Development Plan Outline (2010–2020)" and the "Special Education Promotion Plan (from 2014–2016)". In Tibet, Sichuan, Qinghai, Gansu and other Tibetan regions, special education schools have been established in succession. So far, 14 special education schools have been established in the Tibetan regions of China as a whole. The special education needs of some Tibetan students are being met.

In the survey, we collected the curriculum schedules for deaf and blind students in Ganzi special education schools. To a large extent, those curriculum schedules reflected the basic concept and value orientation of curriculum design for special education in contemporary Tibetan special education schools and fully indicated the development situation of Tibetan special education.

By analysing those curriculum schedules, we can see there are three kinds of courses for 90% of the children with special needs coming from farming and pasturing areas in Tibetan special education schools: (1) cultural knowledge courses, which include languages, maths, science and other basic knowledge; (2) habits and social interaction courses, which intend to cultivate students' etiquette, health habits and communication methods and abilities and (3) living and production skills and specialized courses that aim at helping students learn survival skills by creating their own conditions in their future life.

Special schools in the Tibetan areas are only responsible for compulsory education. After the students complete this education, only a few of them continue their studies in vocational schools or universities, while most have to face the difficulties of transition and placement. So it is necessary to stress the importance of living and producing skills and specialized courses. Depending on the different types of disabled students, many special schools in Tibetan areas have opened some skills courses combining local cultural and social service requirements, such as blind massage for the blind, Tangka painting and tailoring for deaf students, and vocal music, musical instruments and dance for talented students, which can help them obtain some skills for their future life.

By analysing the development of Tibetan special education since 2000, we can draw three conclusions. First, the government is paying considerable attention to the development of Tibetan special education, so more and more children with special needs will get a relatively fair education. However, the few special education schools are far from meeting the requirements of all the children with special needs. Second, although the courses in the Tibetan special education schools meet the national, local and school-based requirements, education in the traditional culture still fails to be fully utilized and sufficient attention fails to be given to the local life of children with special needs. Finally, although special education schools help children with special needs finish compulsory education, there is still no solution for them to transit after early intervention and special education.

Research on special education in the Tibetan areas

Using the CNKI, the Baidu search engine, Google Scholar, ERIC, the E-Book of Palacky University Library, the library of Sichuan Normal University, etc., a total of 35 papers related to Tibetan special education development were found. The focuses of these studies can be summarized as follows:

(1) The current situation of the development of Tibetan special education

As papers such as Chen, Q. M. (2011) "Analysis of the current situation and problems of special education in Tibetan Sichuan"; Dai, H. (2007) "A Study of the Present Situation and Development Strategies of Special Education in Tibet; She, W. B. (2014) "Investigation and Reflection of Special Education in Sichuan Ethnic Areas; Wu, C. Y., Mao, Y. L., & Huang, H. (2014) "Survey on the Development of Special Education Schools in Minority Areas of Sichuan Provinces"; Shen, R. H.(2014) "Research on the Relationship Model of Social Adaptation Social Support and Life Satisfaction of Tibetan Children with a Hearing Loss"; She, W. B. (2014) "Exploring and Analysing the "Three Elements" Model of Vocational Education of Disabled Students Based on the Observation of Disabled Students in Sichuan Special Education Schools". These mainly focus on a formal description of the development of special schools, faculty capacity building and the development of equipment and curriculum design. Some thoughts are also provided on aspects of social investment, family perspectives and traditional culture and their impacts on the development of special education. However, the findings of these academic studies are based on a very limited literature review without empirical field analysis. Therefore, the findings and recommendations of these studies are biased and without in-depth analysis.

Among recent doctoral dissertations, there are two valuable ones, Ge (2014) and Zhou (2015). Ge's "A Comparative Study of Deaf Identity in Chinese Han, Tibetan Regions, and the Czech Republic" compares issues of deaf identity of a majority group, Han, and a minority group, Tibetan, which are explored on the basis of the theory of the Three Levels of Culture; in Zhou's "Research on Tibetan Teachers' Attitudes towards Inclusive Education", the research studies the three-element factors of attitude of the cognitive, emotional and behavioural tendency of Tibetan teachers regarding inclusive education. These two dissertations provide some methodological and theoretical support for this study.

(2) The development of the special education curriculum and teacher capacity in the Tibetan regions

The interventions on the special education development of disabled young Tibetans mainly focus on the development of special schools. The quality of the interventions in the special schools is correlated with the development of the curriculum and teaching quality. Therefore, some studies directed their focuses towards the development of the curriculum and teacher training, for instance, Mei, Z. H. (2014) "Analysis of the Tibetan special education teacher training situation"; "Reflections on the Professional Development of Special Education in Colleges and Universities in Tibet"; Dai, G.Y. (2011) "Research on Teacher Training of Special Education in West China". These studies pointed out that teachers engaged with special education in the Tibetan regions have poor qualifications and the curriculum design does not fit the local conditions. On the basis of these findings, teacher training and curriculum redesign are recommended. However, these proposed measures are mostly at the policy level, or based on the special education development experiences of mainland China, and thus have very limited relevance to the development of special education in the Tibetan regions.

(3) Study of Braille and sign language

The development of Tibetan special education is a recent intervention. The communication skills of deaf and blind teenagers in such areas as Braille and sign language are still at the developing and experimental stage, but in the texts collected for the literature review, there are some studies focused on this aspect, for example Zhong, J. H. et al. (2011) "On Tibetan Language Braille and Its Abbreviations"; Zhao, X. C. (2014) "Initial Research on Tibetan Sign Language: Talking about the Sign Language Work of Ethnic Minorities in China as Well"; Li, H. et al. (2013) "A Cognitive Study of Metaphor and Metonymy of Time in Tibetan Sign Language"; Suo, Q., and Sun, W. Z. (2008) "The development of Tibetan sign language so that there is more Tibetan deaf "barrier-free communication". Research studies in this area are not as popular as those concerning the previous two issues, and their findings mainly focus on the urgent need of incorporating more technical aspects into the community skills in the school curriculum.

Although the aforementioned research studies did not directly address the interventions concerning the development of special education of disabled young people, they represent almost all available research on Tibetan special education. They reflect the various aspects of development issues, educational content and methods and strategies applied, as well as the current situation of the development of special education in the Tibetan regions. In the absence of other direct research materials, these have formed the basis for the study of those rare Tibetan teenagers with disabilities receiving special education interventions. Given the limitations of the existing literature on the development of Tibetan special education, these studies have provided critical information for the research design.

The research and development of special education in foreign countries, mainland China, and Tibetan areas, especially the research and development of early childhood interventions, have been reviewed earlier. Although special education intervention is one of the key terms and concepts in this study, it cannot be found in the relevant literature. Therefore, much space has been given to the definition of and theoretical as well as practical research on the early childhood interventions in order to find some theoretical and methodological basis related to this study. This section has provided a comprehensive and in-depth review of special education in Tibet, which acts as the main focus of this study.

Note

1 This section refers to the Chinese mainland by excluding those regions where ethnic minorities live.

3

VALUES AND CULTURE IN THE TIBETAN ENVIRONMENT FOR SPECIAL EDUCATION

Education as a part of the values

Value theory is a theory that discusses the relationship between the subject and the object. For example, in the Tibetan regions, are the disabled adolescents the subjects or objects of education? If the disabled adolescents are the subjects, what are their needs? If they are the objects, who is the subject? Value theory is an important theory to analyse and describe the value orientation. The value orientation is another important concept of the research. On the basis of understanding and analysis of the value orientation of education in the Tibetan regions, it is a theoretical method to explore the purpose, strategy, method and content of the special education interventions aimed at adolescents with special educational needs. In particular, it clarifies the value of the subject and basic information of its needs and the cultural basis and condition of social identification.

The theoretical basis of special education interventions mainly discusses the supporting theory of the possibility and feasibility of special education interventions aimed at disabled adolescents. Cultural hierarchy theory is a theoretical perspective and logical analytical tool of the research. It is used to analyse the source and level of education of disabled teenagers that need to be understood on a certain cultural basis and under certain social conditions and the basic logic of the historic culture of the judgement of educational value. Hence, the current situation of special education interventions under the value orientation circumstances meeting cultural and social conditions is discussed.

Theory of value

The value theory was generated and developed in the context of value philosophy. Value philosophy is originally an important term used by the neo-Kantian Freiburg School in the late 1890s and early 1900s. It is the basic concept used by Western value philosophers, represented by Windelband and Meinong. In their opinion, the existence of the world may be summed

DOI: 10.4324/9781003268208-3

up as its value. In essence, philosophy is the theory of value. Besides, it is necessary only when it acts as the theory of value (Mu & Wang, 1997). In *Lehrbuch der Geschichte der Philosophie* (in English, *Course of History of Philosophy*), Windelband (1893) pointed out that "philosophy has vital force only when it acts as the value science of universal meaning. Philosophy regards the values of universal meaning as its fields". Zhang Dongsun may be said to have been the first philosopher to try to establish his own philosophical system in modern China, a value-centric philosophical system. He thought that "value is the 'relational essence' between the object and the subject". "Relational essence" simply refers to the idea that "value can only be presented in the relation between the object and the subject. Like alum paper being red after it is soaked in rice water, red is the essence of the relation. . . . [I]t is a natural result of the encounter of the subject and the object" (Zhang, 1934, p. 8). Thinking and mastering the essence of value in terms of the relation between the subject and the object is a relatively comprehensive thought in the understanding of the essence of values in traditional Chinese philosophy. In the Song Dynasty, Zhu Xi really explicitly understood value as a relation and he specifically expressed it. In the discussion of "argumentation" and "lust for gain", he stated:

> the speeches of ancient and modern sages and men of virtue are used to analyse the argumentation, they are carefully read over and over again, and the source of argumentation and the source of lust for gain are thought about constantly; which is more important, which is retained, which is more urgent? At first sight, it seems tasteless. For a long time, the judgment is made. Value evaluation and value selection deal with relations such as affinity, importance, retention and urgency, between the object and the human (the subject). The essence of value is the relation between the subject and the object.
>
> (Zhao, 1991, p. 24)

According to the research findings and methodology of value philosophy, value philosophy may be divided into six categories: subject–object relationship value methodology, human value theory, general value theory or system value theory, natural value theory, value duality theory and phenomenological method value theory of survival theory. The subject–object relationship value methodology has the most results and the greatest influence. It is the main reference value methodology of the research.

For the subject–object relationship value methodology, by the subject–object analysis pattern, the value issue is researched, and the value essence, value category, value existence, value generation process and other issues are revealed. In the research, this pattern of analysis is embodied in the discussion of the value orientation of education meeting the needs for human survival and the exploration of the value orientation of the actual conditions, as well as special education interventions aimed at disabled teenagers that are suitable for this value orientation (Prathap, 2013; Thornberg & Oğuz, 2016).

Theoretical background of special education interventions

From the perspective of the feasibility and necessity of special education interventions, the reference theory suitable for special education interventions in the research mainly includes two categories, namely Lamarck's biological theory (De Lamarck, 2011) and Bandura's theory of social learning (Bandura, 1971).

In the research, the biological theory mainly discusses the organ use and disuse theory and organ compensation or replacement theory. The organ use and disuse theory is a rule in the concept of biological evolutionism put forward by De Lamarck (2011), a French biologist. According to this rule,

> in each animal which does not go beyond its developmental boundary, the relatively frequent continuous use of any organ will gradually enhance this organ, make it developed and expanded, and give a capability in direct proportion to its use; on the contrary, the frequent disuse of any organ will gradually make it weak, the capability increasingly declines, and it disappears finally.

Disabled teenagers are characterized by organ damage or the loss of function in most cases. However, the function of most organs is not completely lost. The residual function can be maintained and developed through educational and training interventions. In other words, through training focused on the relevant organ of disabled teenagers, repeated and frequent training and paying close attention to the training being enjoyable, the organ may not degrade or shrink but may maintain its proper function (Zhang & Yang, 2011).

For the organ function compensation or replacement theory, if a part or an organ of the organism has any pathological change or malfunction, the organism may mobilize the residual capacity of the organ or the capability of other organs to compensate for or replace the lost function through the establishment of new conditions (Zhang & Yang, 2011). According to the observation, after some organ functions are lost, the functioning of other organs of disabled teenagers is especially strong in most cases. For example, although visually impaired teenagers and children lose the visual function, their hearing and touch are more sensitive than those of average people. Through conscious and purposeful educational training and interventions, the visual function may be replaced by the functioning of these organs. Hearing-impaired teenagers often have some residual hearing function, and their hearing function is not completely lost. Through their wearing a hearing aid device and undergoing suitable rehabilitation educational training, the function may be compensated for.

If the organ use and disuse theory and organ function compensation or replacement theory are the important theoretical basis for possible special education interventions aimed at disabled teenagers, the social learning theory is the important theoretical basis for the feasibility of special education interventions aimed at disabled teenagers.

The social learning theory emerged in the 1960s and was originated by Bandura (1971). In the social learning theory, he suggests that social learning is the process in which an individual masters the social knowledge, experience and code of conduct and skills to meet their social needs. It may be divided into observational learning and experience-based learning. Observational learning is the process in which the individual obtains similar behaviour by observing the response behaviour of a model. Experience-based learning is the process in which the individual responds directly to a stimulus and obtains information from the resulting response. Observational learning and experience-based learning are very common ways of learning in society. Bandura conducted tremendous experimental research on these two kinds of social learning and revealed the law. This provides technical and theoretical support for special education interventions aimed at disabled teenagers. For example, he stresses learning by imitation and the vicarious reinforcement role of the model. These contents are embodied in special education interventions. In many cases, special education interventions let children with special needs learn the corresponding behaviour by imitation through the demonstration activity of the teacher. Additionally, in the social learning theory, the self-regulation ability of the individual is emphasized. Though the self-regulation ability of disabled teenagers may be poorer than that of intact teenagers, they also have autonomy. In many special education interventions, the teachers will bring the forces of the teenagers into play to promote the effects of the special education intervention. These methods and concepts cannot operate without the support of social learning theory.

Theoretical background of cultural hierarchy

As culture is not an important concept in this research, its definitions will not be discussed here. However, in the analysis of value orientation and the discussion of special education interventions under a certain value orientation, cultural analysis is required. In particular, the cultural hierarchy theory is suitable as the theoretical method used in the research. Therefore, the cultural hierarchy theory and the cultural structure hierarchy theory model built in the research are discussed in the following text.

Hofstede's Onion Theory and Schein's Organizational Culture have great influences on the cultural hierarchy theory.

Hofstede's onion theory of culture

Hofstede, a social psychologist from the Netherlands, is famous for his pioneering research on cross-cultural groups and organizations. In 1980, Hofstede first created the model of the "Cultural Onion" on the basis of abundant surveys and collected data in his book "Culture's consequences: comparing values, behaviours, institutions, and organization across nations" (Hofstede, 2001). He thinks that the cultural hierarchy may be clearly summarized when four terms, namely symbol, hero, etiquette and value, are combined. He compares culture to an onion. The level of culture is several layers of the onion. "Symbol" is the outermost surface layer, "value" is the innermost expression form and "hero" and "etiquette" are in the middle. Therefore, his cultural hierarchy theory is also called the "cultural onion peel theory". Some symbols are words, some are practices and some are charts or objects. These phenomena have their specific meanings. Only a person who shares a culture can identify these. The symbols of a cultural group are often imitated by other groups, so symbols are in the outermost layer. The features of a "hero" are extolled or praised in a certain culture, so it becomes the model for behaviour. "Etiquette" relates to collective activity, such as social contact ceremonies, religious rites and commercial and political assemblies. Symbols, heroes and etiquette are put into "practice", and they may be observed by the outside world. However, their cultural significance is intangible, and it is definitely manifested by the people in this cultural circle through their practice. The cultural core is composed of values. Value is the basic belief and value orientation followed by people. It is an emotion of pointing to positive or negative by an arrow, such as kindness and evil, beauty and ugliness and compliance with natural law and violations of natural law.

Schein's model of organizational culture

A former professor of the Alfred P. Sloan School of Management of Massachusetts Institute of Technology, Schein created a model of organizational culture, namely "Three Levels of Culture", in the 1980s. Schein (2010) identifies three distinct levels in organizational cultures: artefacts, espoused values and basic assumptions and values. He believes that culture is composed of the following three interactive levels:

- Material level: observed organizational structures and organizational processes, etc.
- Supporting value: including strategy, goals, quality awareness, guidance philosophy, etc.
- Basic subconsciousness assumption: some subconscious beliefs, consciousness, thoughts, feelings, etc.

The position and relations of these three levels are clearly shown through the shape used in the Cultural Onion Theory.

The material level is the surface of a certain culture. It is easily identified but hard to understand. The support value is the value and code of conduct stated in the organization. The basic subconsciousness assumption involves deep-rooted and accepted behaviours, and these behaviours are generally unconscious but constitute the essence of the culture.

The difference between the Cultural Onion theory and Organizational Culture theory is obvious. On the basis of different cultural dimensions, they analyse the structure of a culture and emphasize the relationship between different dimensions.

The theory of four levels of culture in the present research

Influenced and inspired by the aforementioned cultural hierarchy theory, the research builds the four levels of the cultural theory according to the theoretical model of "life understanding of identity culture" of Nima and Liu (2016) and this method of educational analysis based on a cultural hierarchy.

Beliefs: Belief based on Tibetan culture and Tibetan social needs.

Values: Educational value orientation based on Tibetan culture and actual social conditions. Namely values and value standards manifested in the judgement, education, implementation and evaluation of education.

Behaviours: Specific activity of special education interventions aimed at disabled teenagers that meet the value orientation of education in the Tibetan regions: purpose of the intervention, content of the intervention, intervention method and strategy.

Institutions: Organization that supports the special education interventions aimed at disabled teenagers in the Tibetan regions: School, Family and Community.

By means of these structural levels, the special education intervention of disabled teenagers from the perspective of the value orientation in the Tibetan regions is analysed.

Culture is a structure with four concentric levels that enables an understanding of life, and the belief level, value level, behavioural level and organizational level exist, respectively, from inside to outside.

The deepest level of this model is belief, in other words, the core structure of the culture. Belief is the understanding of life. To be specific, it is the answer of an ethnic group (or people in the same culture) to the understanding of life and death. This answer is the origin of their cultural world and the source of their needs. Additionally, it is the origin of the values by which a person judges and analyses things. The outlook on time and space depends on the outlook on life. Everything involved in the human life is the understanding of time and space according to belief. The need is generated, and it is the need for a human being to understand life (namely to answer the questions of life and death). This level is used to analyse the people's belief on the basis of Tibetan society and culture, discuss the educational need for the understanding of life and explore suitable special education interventions aimed at disabled teenagers. Values are the judgement of "the true, the good, and the beautiful". Values grow on the basis of belief and satisfy needs. They are used to analyse the value orientation of education, which has a certain cultural basis and social reality. The behavioural level is the behaviour that meets various needs. It is used to analyse the behaviours and activities of special education interventions aimed at disabled teenagers. The organizational level is the organization to guarantee the implementation of various activities. It discusses how to establish the school, family, community and other organizations suitable for special education interventions aimed at disabled teenagers in the Tibetan regions.

4

PERCEPTION AND ATTITUDE OF LEARNING

We have to start with three major areas which are interesting from the focus of education and its value in the Tibetan area.

1 The origin of value orientation and its alternative purpose of special education for children in the Tibetan areas through a cultural perspective in order to explore the theoretical, methodological and practical implementation strategies for the development of Tibetan special education.
2 Systematize the alternative purpose of school education by comparing the value orientation of special education and general school education in Tibetan areas.
3 Complex methods and strategies of special education interventions aimed at adolescents with disabilities on the basis of the value orientation of Tibetan special education and the purpose of the analysis.

Education is a lifelong process, and its function is to continuously improve people's ability to deal with and use a range of knowledge. The purpose of the teaching process is to stimulate enjoyment and create a journey towards wisdom, and education aims to make everyone live with dignity. This is the cognitive basis of the research on the subject, and education for adolescents with a disability is no exception. On the basis of the investigation and analysis of knowledge about people's attitudes towards education and the choice of educational value, basic methods are required to answer the questions raised in the research. Therefore, the present study adopted the methodology of combining qualitative and quantitative research.

The path of qualitative research

As a field of inquiry in the human sciences, qualitative research has a long and distinguished history (Denzin & Lincoln, 1994). Qualitative research is an activity that considers the researchers themselves as a research tool and performs an in-depth and comprehensive study on phenomena, forms

DOI: 10.4324/9781003268208-4

conclusions and theories from original data and obtains an interpretive understanding of the behaviour and construction of meaning by interacting with the targets on the basis of multiple data collection methods (interviews, observations and analyses of objects) in a natural setting. A literature review, interviews and case studies are mainly used for the research.

As far as the research is concerned, documents of several types need to be carefully collected and analysed: first, classical Tibetan works (including literature, history, Buddhism and others) to learn about the value orientation of education in traditional Tibetan culture; second, earlier relevant research documents on special education interventions and the implementation and methods of special education in the Tibetan areas to obtain research theories and methods for reference purposes; third, policies and regulations, clauses of documents and various documents from communities and service organizations for disabled persons to learn about China's legal protection and social support for special education in the Tibetan areas; and last, documents on school management, student training objectives and curriculum design and implementation at special education schools in the Tibetan areas.

An interview is a useful method for collecting data in a qualitative research study. The research intends to conduct in-depth semi-structured interviews with monks, students, teachers and parents from general and special education schools. In the Tibetan areas, monks who accept a traditional education are typical representatives of the traditional values in Tibetan culture. The main purpose of the interviews with them is, on the one hand, to understand the value orientation in traditional Tibetan culture and their recognition of traditional Tibetan education and, on the other hand, to understand the attitude towards current education from the point of view of traditional cultural values.

Narrative research methods: Most case study research is interpretive and seeks to bring a case to life. It often, but not exclusively, occurs in a natural setting, and it may employ qualitative and/or quantitative methods and measures (Anderson, 2005, p. 161). The narrative research in this study mainly includes narrative case studies and narrative journals kept by the researcher while surveying Tibetan special education schools. These narrative resources are used to further analyse the status quo and problems of the development of special education in the Tibetan regions. They may inspire thought and discussion on interventions in the special education of disabled adolescents in the Tibetan regions.

The path of quantitative research

Questionnaire surveys: Questionnaires have become one of the most used and abused means of collecting information (Anderson & Arsenault, 2005). Compared to a literature search, the approach used in collecting data is a prominent feature of questionnaire surveys (Wiersma & Jurs, 2010), which usually get information from the respondent group with a certain paper-and-pencil instrument. In this study, questionnaires were designed to investigate the value orientation of education in the Tibetan regions. The focus is on the educational concepts of students, parents and teachers in regular middle schools and special education schools, as well as their understanding, evaluation and choices of education. There are three types of questionnaires for different subject groups: students, parents and teachers. There are 20 identical core questions in each questionnaire. They were used in our previous research project about the value of special education in the Tibetan regions. In addition to these 20 core questions, the questionnaire also includes questions about information on the respondents and their basic attitudes. There are four optional questions asking about the factors that greatly influence the educational concepts of students, in addition to the 20 required core questions. The subjects have to answer Yes or No. In the questionnaires for parents, three more questions ask about their satisfaction with, and expectations about, the education their child is receiving. Five questions are added to the questionnaires for teachers to ascertain their satisfaction with the existing education and their recognition of the knowledge and skills that the students are learning. The questionnaires are translated into Tibetan and Chinese so that they can be easily understood by the respondents.

Two aspects need to be considered when choosing the questionnaire samples. The first one is that the Tibetan areas can be divided by ways of production into farming, pastoral and farming-pastoral areas. In addition, quite a number of Tibetan people are urban residents who work in schools, offices, etc. So the samples should cover the populations in all areas; the second is that teachers, students and parents in general schools and special education schools should be selected as questionnaire respondents.

Statistical methods: This study uses a descriptive statistical method to analyse the attitudes and views on education of different groups of people. It also focuses on their opinions on education in order to describe the current value orientation of education in the Tibetan areas and the special education interventions aimed at disabled adolescents there.

The processing of the questionnaire data is an important quantitative approach in this study. All the questionnaire data to be acquired were encoded and recorded into the statistical programme SPSS (Statistical Package for Social Sciences). The central tendency will be observed by means and medians; the questionnaire results will be analysed and described by statistical methods based on frequency distribution and percentages. The core variables are described by the exploratory factor method. In order to understand if there are differences in attitudes to education between different demographic groups of respondents, the study uses the method of one-way analysis of variance (ANOVA) to examine it.

In addition to the aforementioned methods, the research will also analyse the research contents and materials using the cultural stratification theory, the cultural self-reflection theory and the constructivist learning theory. It is an attempt to construct an educational analysis theory based on value and value orientation.

To sum up, Figure 4.1 illustrates the system of the research methods of the present study.

Areas of investigation

In terms of their administrative division, the Tibetan people are mainly distributed in the TAR, Sichuan Province, Qinghai Province, Gansu Province and Yunnan Province. In the research, after the comprehensive consideration of population distribution, economic development status, research conditions and other factors, the city of Lhasa and Rikaze Prefecture and Sn Prefecture in Tibet, Ganzi Tibetan Autonomous Prefecture and Aba Tibetan and Qiang Autonomous Prefectures in Sichuan Province, Ys Tibetan

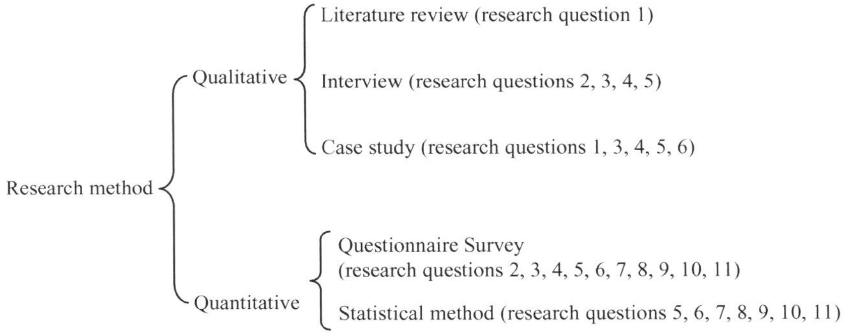

Figure 4.1 The system of the research methods of the present study

Table 4.1 Areas of investigation of this research

Code	*Province Region*	*City/Prefecture*
1	Tibetan Autonomous Region	Lhasa City
2		Sn Region
3		Rikaze Region
4	Sichuan Province	Ganzi Tibetan Autonomous Prefecture
5		Aba Tibetan and Qiang Autonomous Prefecture
6		Chengdu No. 3 Middle School
7	Qinghai Province	Ys Tibetan Autonomous Prefecture
8	Gansu Province	Gannan Autonomous Prefecture

Autonomous Prefecture in Qinghai Province and Gannan Tibetan Autonomous Prefecture in Gansu Province were selected. Tibetan students from No. 3 Middle School of Chengdu, Sichuan Province, were also selected in the sample of respondents (Table 4.1).

The region surveyed is described earlier in simple terms. Basic information on the composition of the people participating in the questionnaires, interviews and the like will be introduced in the chapters and sections in which the corresponding survey results are analysed.

5

RESULTS AND CONCLUSION

Results of the questionnaire survey

Since there are three types of samples in this research, namely students, parents and teachers, three types of questionnaires are designed correspondingly. Each questionnaire includes three parts: questions seeking basic information about the samples, core questions and questions aimed at gaining an understanding of the basic attitudes of the respondents. The three types of questionnaires share the same core questions from Q1 to Q20 on a scale from 1 to 5: strongly agree, agree, I don't know, disagree and strongly disagree. There are four questions asking about the basic attitudes of students, from Q21 to Q24, with two options: 1 for yes and 2 for no. There are three questions asking about the basic attitudes of parents, from Q21 to Q23, with the scale and value assignment the same as with the core questions. There are five questions asking about the basic attitudes of teachers, from Q21 to Q25, with the scale and value assignment the same as with the core questions. The statistics and analysis of the survey results from the three sample groups appear in the following.

Results of the questionnaire survey for students

(1) Gender of students

The distribution objects of the student questionnaire are lower secondary school and upper secondary school students of special education schools and general schools in the Tibetan regions. The way of distribution was face to face, sampled in the class in the school that was surveyed. The questionnaires were completed in July to November 2017. A total of 700 questionnaires were distributed and all were returned. After questionnaires missing basic data had been excluded, there were 670 valid ones: a total of 670 students responding with effective questionnaires, including 522 students from the general school, accounting for 77.9% of the respondents, and 148 students from the special education school, accounting for 22.1% of the

DOI: 10.4324/9781003268208-5

Table 5.1 Statistics for students' gender (N = 670)

Different background factors		*Sample size (person)*	*Percentage (%)*
Gender	Male	277	41.3
	Female	393	58.7

Table 5.2 Statistics for students' ages (N = 670)

Different background factors		*Sample size (people)*	*Percentage (%)*
Age	9–12 years	20	3.0
	13–18 years	627	93.6
	19–20 years	22	3.3
	Missing	1	0.1

respondents. The background information on the students who were surveyed is as follows (Table 5.1 and Table 5.2).

Basic situation of students in the questionnaire

(2) Age status of students

Among the 670 students in the questionnaire, there were 277 boys, accounting for 41.3% of the respondents, and 393 girls, accounting for 58.7% of the respondents.

Regarding the students participating in the questionnaire, there are 20 students from 9 to 12 years old, and there are 22 students from 19 to 20 years old. These samples come from the special education school. This is inconsistent with the requirement of the student respondents being from 13 to 18 years old in the research. However, most special education schools in the Tibetan regions have only been established for a few years. The age range of the students who were recruited is from 6 to 26 years old. Among the students from 13 to 18 years old in the same class, there are not a few students below 13 years old and above 18 years old. Considering the actual situation, in the statistical analysis, the questionnaires of these 42 students are included among the valid questionnaires (Table 5.3).

(3) Educational background of students

The general students in the questionnaire are lower secondary school students or upper secondary school students but not the students of special

Table 5.3 Statistics for educational background of students ($N = 670$)

Different Background Factors		*Sample Size (person)*	*Percentage (%)*
Education	Lower secondary school	293	43.7
	Upper secondary school	296	44.2
	Primary school	81	12.1

education schools. As special schools in the Tibetan regions are rather new, many only have primary school students. However, students in most special schools are over-aged, and many of them are between 13 and 18 years old.

Reliability and validity analysis

(1) Reliability analysis

"Reliability" refers to the authenticity and reliability of research data and is about whether the respondents answer each question truthfully (Zhou, 2017, p. 43). Cronbach's alpha statistics are shown in Table 5.4.

According to Cronbach's alpha statistics for the questionnaire shown earlier, it is found that Cronbach's alpha is greater than 0.7, which indicates excellent validity of the questionnaire, so it meets the requirements of this research.

(2) Validity analysis

"Validity" is the effective expression of the conceptual information about variables in the questions. It is about whether the questions and scales are designed reasonably (Zhou, 2017, p. 44). Validity analysis mainly includes content validity analysis and structural validity analysis. The questionnaires in this research were used in a study on the value of special education in the Tibetan regions. Therefore, the content validity is not tested again in this research. Exploratory factor analysis is adopted to analyse the structural validity of the 20 core questions. The result shows that all the questions have a factor loading coefficient over 0.4, except Q19, whose factor loading coefficient is 0.37. Thus, all of the 20 core questions are retained. The factor loading coefficients are analysed in Table 5.5.

The 20 questions are analysed with exploratory factor analysis. Table 5.6 shows the KMO value of 0.858, much greater than 0.7. Bartlett's test of sphericity yields a P-value of 0.000. These data indicate that the questionnaire has good structural validity and meets the requirements for further factor analysis.

Table 5.4 Cronbach's alpha statistics for the student questionnaire

Cronbach's alpha	*No. of Items*
0.791	24

Table 5.5 Cumulative analysis of the student questionnaire

Item	*Initial*	*Extraction*
Higher education = good job security.	1.000	0.509
Education is the path to success at work.	1.000	0.512
Education protects humans against poverty.	1.000	0.480
Education is increasingly a guarantee of a higher income.	1.000	0.527
Education encourages entrepreneurial activity.	1.000	0.471
Highly educated people make up the nation's elite.	1.000	0.405
It is worthwhile to go abroad for a good education.	1.000	0.505
Schools are not required.	1.000	0.710
The main thing is a diploma.	1.000	0.639
Contacts are important.	1.000	0.534
Education in my country is a waste of time.	1.000	0.516
Being able to work is the most important thing.	1.000	0.555
One may make a good living without education.	1.000	0.560
Most people should have an education.	1.000	0.541
You cannot build a career without education.	1.000	0.471
Professionalism is more important than education.	1.000	0.721
Work will show up.	1.000	0.550
Education can be afforded only by those who have the money for it.	1.000	0.565
Graduation is required.	1.000	0.370
An educated person need not worry about not finding work.	1.000	0.536

Table 5.6 KMO and Bartlett's test results for the student questionnaire

Kaiser-Meyer-Olkin Measure of Sampling Adequacy		0.858
Bartlett's test of sphericity	Appor. chi-square	2,278.385
	Df	190
	Sig.	0.000

Table 5.6 shows that for the 20 core questions in this questionnaire, six factors are automatically extracted by the method of factor extraction of principal components. The cumulative variance interpretation rate is 53.388%, and the total variance interpretation rate is greater than 50% (Table 5.7). Overall, it shows that the exploratory factor result analysis is acceptable.

Table 5.7 Total variance of the student questionnaire explained ($N = 670$)

Compo-nent	*Initial Eigenvalues*			*Extraction of Squared Loadings*			*Rotation Sums of Squared Loadings*
	Total	*% of Variance*	*Cumulative %*	*Total*	*% of Variance*	*Cumulative %*	*Total*
1	4.296	21.482	21.482	4.296	21.482	21.482	2.893
2	2.064	10.322	31.805	2.064	10.322	31.805	2.711
3	1.380	6.899	38.704	1.380	6.899	38.704	1.400
4	1.302	5.158	43.862	1.032	5.158	43.862	1.258
5	.988	4.938	48.800	.988	4.938	48.800	1.216
6	.918	4.588	53.388	.918	4.588	53.388	1.198
7	.899	4.494	57.881				
8	.840	4.199	62.081				
9	.817	4.084	66.164				
. . .							

Table 5.8 Items relating to each of the factors

	Item
Factor score 1	Education can be afforded only by those who have the money for it.
	Work will show up.
	Education in my country is a waste of time.
	An educated person need not worry about not finding work.
	You cannot build a career without education.
	Graduation is required.
Factor score 2	Education is the path to success at work.
	Education is increasingly a guarantee of a higher income.
	Education protects humans against poverty.
	Higher education = good job security.
	Highly educated people make up the nation's elite.
	Education encourages entrepreneurial activity.
Factor score 3	Contacts are important.
	It is worthwhile to go abroad for a good education.
Factor score 4	Being able to work is the most important thing.
	The main thing is a diploma.
Factor score 5	Professionalism is more important than education.
	Most people should have an education.
Factor score 6	Schools are not required.
	One may make a good living without education.

According to the score analysis of the "rotated component matrix", the items relating to each of the six factors are shown in Table 5.8.

On the basis of the items relating to each factor and the investigation and survey on the educational concept of students and their educational viewpoints in this research, the following naming interpretation is performed for the six factors.

Factor 1: Education is needed to get a good job.
Factor 2: The level of education determines employment and careers.
Factor 3: Diplomas from abroad and contacts are important for employment.
Factor 4: Education is needed but the ability to work and contacts are more important.
Factor 5: Education is needed and is a way of gaining social recognition.
Factor 6: For good work, contacts and entrepreneurial spirit are enough. Education is better abroad.

Results of the questionnaire

(1) Mean, median, minimum, maximum and standard deviation of the questionnaire

In the statistics mentioned earlier, for Q1, Q2, Q3, Q4, Q5, Q6, Q7, Q8, Q9, Q10, Q12, Q14 and Q16, the mean value is less than 3.00 and the median is 2.00. This shows that more than 50% of the respondents accept these statements. For Q11, Q18 and Q20, the mean value is greater than 3.00 and the median is 4.00. This shows that more than 50% of the respondents do not accept these statements. For the remaining questions, Q13, Q15, Q17 and Q19, the median is 3. This shows that the percentage of the respondents who chose the answer "I do not know" to these statements is less than 50% (Table 5.9).

(2) Selected phenomena with significant frequency

Among the 20 core questions, those with higher frequencies are shown in Table 5.10.

In this table, the result "agree" is the sum of "strongly agree" and "agree". The result "disagree" is the sum of "disagree" and "strongly disagree". According to the statistics, of the 20 questions, most students agreed that "Education is the path to success at work" (74.2%), "Education encourages entrepreneurial activity" (73.3%) and "Most people should have an education" (76.5%). They mostly disagreed with the statements "Education in my country is a waste of time" (61.7%) and "Education can be afforded only by those who have the money for it" (62.7%). The largest percentage of students who gave the answer "I do not know" appears for "Highly educated people make up the nation's elite" (27.8%), "One may make a

Table 5.9 Descriptive statistics for main items measuring variance

Measuring Item	*N*		*Mean*	*Median*	*Minimum*	*Maximum*	*Std. Deviation*
	Valid	*Missing*					
Q1	670	0	2.38	2.00	1	5	1.067
Q2	666	4	2.08	2.00	1	5	0.890
Q3	669	1	2.42	2.00	1	5	1.048
Q4	668	2	2.56	2.00	1	5	1.078
Q5	666	4	2.15	2.00	1	5	0.900
Q6	668	2	2.49	2.00	1	5	1.027
Q7	669	1	2.44	2.00	1	5	1.137
Q8	668	2	2.51	2.00	1	5	1.143
Q9	667	3	2.19	2.00	1	5	0.996
Q10	667	3	2.17	2.00	1	5	1.119
Q11	665	5	3.65	4.00	1	5	1.345
Q12	668	2	2.7	2.00	1	5	1.176
Q13	669	1	2.86	3.00	1	5	1.139
Q14	669	1	2.05	2.00	1	5	1.013
Q15	669	1	2.87	3.00	1	5	1.126
Q16	667	3	2.63	2.00	1	5	1.076
Q17	668	2	3.27	3.00	1	5	1.247
Q18	668	2	3.63	4.00	1	5	1.274
Q19	667	3	3.20	3.00	1	5	1.328
Q20	669	1	3.30	4.00	1	5	1.224

Table 5.10 The items with significant frequency

Statement	*Item*	*Frequency and Percentage*
Agree	Education is the path to success at work.	494 (74.2%)
	Education encourages entrepreneurial activity.	488 (73.3%)
	Most people should have an education.	512 (76.5%)
Disagree	Education in my country is a waste of time.	413 (61.7%)
	Education can be afforded only by those who have the money for it.	422 (62.7%)
I do not know	Highly educated people make up the nation's elite.	186 (27.8%)
	One may make a good living without education.	182 (27.2%)
	You cannot build a career without education.	191 (28.5%)

good living without education" (27.2%) and "You cannot build a career without education" (28.5%).

(3) Items relating to basic attitudes

There are four items that relate to basic attitudes. The results can be described in terms of frequency.

The biggest influence on my ideas about education is from my family.

Among the students who were surveyed, 545, accounting for 81.3% of the respondents, stated that their educational concept and viewpoint are greatly influenced by their family (parents); 115 students, accounting for 17.2% of the respondents, stated that their educational concept is not influenced by their family (shown in Table 5.11). Ten students failed to give an answer.

The biggest influence on my ideas about education is from the school.

Among the students who were surveyed, 513 students, accounting for 76.6% of the respondents, stated that their educational concept and viewpoint are greatly influenced by the school; 148 students, accounting for 22.1% of the respondents, stated that their educational concept is not influenced by the school (see Table 5.12). Nine students failed to give an answer.

The biggest influence on my ideas about education is from my friends.

As shown in Table 5.13 among the students who were surveyed, 347 students, accounting for 51.8% of the respondents, stated that their educational

Table 5.11 Statistics for Item A on basic attitudes

	Frequency	*Percentage*	*Valid Percentage*	*Cumulative Percentage*
Valid YES	545	81.3	82.6	82.6
NO	115	517.2		100.0
Total	660	98.5	100.0	
Answer missing	10	1.5		
Total	670	100.0		

Table 5.12 Statistics for Item B on basic attitudes

	Frequency	*Percentage*	*Valid Percentage*	*Cumulative Percentage*
Valid YES	513	76.6	77.6	77.6
NO	148	22.1	22.4	100.0
Total	661	98.7	100.0	
Answer missing	9	1.3		
Total	670	100.0		

Table 5.13 Statistics for Item C on basic attitudes

	Frequency	*Percentage*	*Valid Percentage*	*Cumulative Percentage*
Valid YES	347	51.8	52.7	52.7
NO	312	46.6	47.3	100.0
Total	659	98.4	100.3	
Answer missing	11	1.6		
Total	670	100.0		

Table 5.14 Statistics for Item D on basic attitudes

	Frequency	*Percentage*	*Valid Percentage*	*Cumulative Percentage*
Valid YES	288	43.0	43.5	43.5
NO	374	55.8	56.5	100.0
Total	662	98.8	100.0	
Answer missing	8	1.2		
Total	670	100.0		

concept and viewpoint are greatly influenced by their friends; 312 students, accounting for 46.6% of the respondents, stated that their educational concept is not influenced by their friends. Eleven students failed to answer this question.

The biggest influence on my ideas about education is from the media.

Among the students who were surveyed, 288 students, accounting for 43.0% of the respondents, stated that their educational concept and viewpoint are greatly influenced by the media; 374 students, accounting for 55.8% of the respondents, stated that their educational concept is not influenced by the media (see Table 5.14). Eight students failed to answer this question.

(4) Demographic differences between the student questionnaire respondents

Gender differences

In order to understand if there are differences in ideas about education between students of different genders, the study takes the method of one-way ANOVA to examine it; the results are shown in Table 5.15.

According to the analysis of the gender differences between the students, it is found that the factor “Education is needed to get a good job” is the one most affected by all the different factors so as to become a significant

Table 5.15 The results of the ANOVA of the students by gender

		Sum of Squares	*df*	*Mean Square*	*F*	*Sig.*
REGR factor score 1 for analysis 1	Between Groups	6.555	1	6.555	6.612	.010
	Within Groups	648.445	654	0.992		
	Total	655.000	655			
REGR factor score 2 for analysis 1	Between Groups	0.001	1	0.001	.001	.973
	Within Groups	654.999	654	1.002		
	Total	655.000	655			
REGR factor score 3 for analysis 1	Between Groups	0.562	1	0.562	.562	.454
	Within Groups	654.438	654	1.001		
	Total	655.000	655			
REGR factor score 4 for analysis 1	Between Groups	0.000	1	0.000	.000	.990
	Within Groups	655.000	654	1.002		
	Total	655.000	655			
REGR factor score 5 for analysis 1	Between Groups	.470	1	0.470	.469	.494
	Within Groups	654.530	654	1.001		
	Total	655.000	655			
REGR factor score 6 for analysis 1	Between Groups	0.288	1	0.288	.288	.592
	Within Groups	654.172	654	1.001		
	Total	655.000	655			

difference. However, there was no statistical significance in the factors "The level of education determines employment and careers", "Diplomas from abroad and contacts are important for employment", "Education is needed but the ability to work and contacts are more important", "Education is needed and is a way of gaining social recognition" and "For good work, contacts and entrepreneurial spirit are enough. Education is better abroad".

A further analysis was performed with a comparison of the means between groups. The factor "Education is needed to get a good job" that more boys than girls think that a good job is inextricably connected with education. The schoolboys pay more attention to whether a good and satisfactory job can be obtained through receiving education. However, with regard to job quality, the schoolgirls do not have higher requirements than the boys. The girls think that finding a bread-winning job will be possible by receiving education.

Age group differences

In order to understand if there are differences in terms of their ideas about education between students in different age groups, the study takes the method of one-way ANOVA to examine it; the results are shown in Table 5.16.

The analysis of the differences has shown that the *p*-value is greater than the level of significance, that is Sig > 0.05. Therefore, there are no significant

Table 5.16 The results of the ANOVA of the students by age

		Sum of Squares	*df*	*Mean Square*	*F*	*Sig.*
REGR factor score 1 for analysis 1	Between Groups	1.029	2	0.515	.513	.599
	Within Groups	651.913	650	1.003		
	Total	652.942	652			
REGR factor score 2 for analysis 1	Between Groups	.785	2	0.393	.394	.674
	Within Groups	647.512	650	0.996		
	Total	648.306	652			
REGR factor score 3 for analysis 1	Between Groups	4.522	2	2.261	2.267	.104
	Within Groups	68.365	650	0.988		
	Total	652.752	652			
REGR factor score 4 for analysis 1	Between Groups	4.673	2	2.336	2.340	.097
	Within Groups	649.080	650	0.999		
	Total	653.752	652			
REGR factor score 5 for analysis 1	Between Groups	1.020	2	0.510	.511	.600
	Within Groups	649.159	650	0.988		
	Total	650.179	652			
REGR factor score 6 for analysis 1	Between Groups	.199	2	0.099	.099	.906
	Within Groups	651.691	650	1.003		
	Total	651.889	652			

differences between the students' ideas about education in terms of their age group.

Differences due to educational background

In order to understand if there are differences in ideas about education between students from different schools, the study takes the method of one-way ANOVA to examine it, with the results shown in Table 5.17.

Through the analysis of the different schools attended by the students, it is found that the factors "Education is needed to get a good job" and "The level of education determines employment and careers" are those most affected by all the different factors so as to become significant differences. However, there was no statistical significance in the factors "A diploma from abroad and contacts are important for employment", "Education is needed but the ability to work and contacts are more important", "Education is needed and is a way of attaining social recognition" and "For good work, contacts and entrepreneurial spirit are enough. Education is better abroad".

A further analysis was performed with a comparison of the means between groups. The factor "Education is needed to get a good job" is that the lower secondary school students place the most value on the relationship between a good job and education, similarly is followed by the primary school pupils.

Table 5.17 The results of the ANOVA of the students by educational background

		Sum of Squares	*df*	*Mean Square*	*F*	*Sig.*
REGR factor score 1 for analysis 1	Between Groups	54.573	2	27.286	29.676	.000
	Within Groups	600.427	653	0.919		
	Total	655.000	655			
REGR factor score 2 for analysis 1	Between Groups	28.553	2	14.276	14.882	.000
	Within Groups	626.447	653	0.959		
	Total	655.000	655			
REGR factor score 3 for analysis 1	Between Groups	1.485	2	0.743	.742	.477
	Within Groups	653.515	653	1.001		
	Total	655.000	655			
REGR factor score 4 for analysis 1	Between Groups	0.802	2	0.401	.400	.670
	Within Groups	654.198	653	1.002		
	Total	655.000	655			
REGR factor score 5 for analysis 1	Between Groups	2.532	2	1.262	1.263	.284
	Within Groups	652.477	653	.999		
	Total	655.000	655			
REGR factor score 6 for analysis 1	Between Groups	1.967	2	.984	.984	.374
	Within Groups	653.033	653	1.000		
	Total	655.000	655			

However, the upper secondary school students do not see this relationship in the same way. This is related to the college entrance examination, a demanding task for them; the sole goal of upper secondary school students is to be admitted to a university. With regard to the factor "The level of education determines employment and careers", the upper secondary school students regard it as less important in comparison with the lower secondary school students and the primary school pupils. Like in the previous analysis, this is still related to the short-term goal of pursuing college enrolment in upper secondary school education.

Results of the questionnaire survey for parents

Questionnaires were also distributed to the parents of the lower and upper secondary school students in special education schools and general schools in the selected regions mentioned earlier. The questionnaires were distributed and collected in person from July to November 2017. A total of 250 questionnaires were distributed and 235 were returned; the recovery rate was 94%. Questionnaires with missing basic information and those suspected of plagiarism were excluded so that 211 valid questionnaires filled out by 211 parents remained; 159 of them were parents of regular school students, accounting for 75.4% of the total parent sample; 52 of them were parents of students from special education schools, accounting for 24.6%. What follows is the basic information about these parents, their responses and the analysis.

Situation of parents in the questionnaire

Of the 211 parents responding to the questionnaire, 131 were fathers, accounting for 62.1% of the respondents, and 80 were mothers, accounting for 37.9%. There were considerably more fathers than mothers participating in the survey (shown in Table 5.18).

Table 5.19 shows that there were 93 parents aged 30–39, accounting for 44% of the respondents, 99 parents aged 40–49, accounting for 47% of the respondents, and 19 parents aged over 50 years, accounting for 9% of the respondents. The largest number of parents was in the 40–49 age group, and those aged over 50 were the smallest group.

Of the parents surveyed, 82 were illiterate, accounting for 38.9%; 100 were lower secondary school graduates, accounting for 47.4%; 15 were upper secondary school graduates, accounting for 7.1%; five were vocational school graduates, accounting for 2.4%; nine were university graduates,

Table 5.18 Statistics for parents' gender (N = 211)

Different Background Factors		*Sample Size (Person)*	*Percentage (%)*
(1) Gender of parents			
Gender	Male	132	62.6
	Female	79	37.4

Table 5.19 Statistics for age status of parents (N = 211)

Different Background Factors		*Sample Size (Person)*	*Percentage (%)*
(2) Age status of parents			
Age	30–39 years	93	44
	40–49 years	99	47
	50 years and above	19	9

accounting for 4.3%. The statistics show that most of the parents over 30 had low levels of education and had received little education in the Tibetan regions (as shown in Table 5.20).

Reliability and validity analysis

(1) RELIABILITY ANALYSIS

The statistics for Cronbach's alpha are shown in Table 5.21.

According to the statistics for Cronbach's alpha of the questionnaire mentioned earlier, it is found that Cronbach's alpha is greater than 0.7, which indicates excellent validity of the questionnaire, which means that it meets the requirement of this research.

(2) VALIDITY ANALYSIS

Exploratory factor analysis is adopted to analyse the structural validity of the 20 core questions. The result shows that all the questions have a factor loading coefficient over 0.4, except Q19, whose factor loading coefficient is 0.354. Thus, all of the 20 core questions are retained. The factor loading coefficients are analysed in Table 5.22.

The 20 questions are analysed with exploratory factor analysis. Table 5.23 shows the KMO value of 0.782, much greater than 0.7. The Bartlett's test of sphericity yields a *P*-value of 0.000. These data indicate that the

Table 5.20 Statistics for educational background status of parents (N = 211)

Different Background Factors		*Sample Size (Person)*	*Percentage (%)*
(3) Educational background of parents			
Education	Illiteracy	82	38.9
	Lower secondary school	100	47.4
	Upper secondary school	15	7.1
	Vocational school	5	2.4
	university	9	4.3

Table 5.21 Statistics for Cronbach's alpha of the questionnaire for parents

Cronbach's Alpha	*No. of Items*
0.821	23

Table 5.22 Cumulative analysis of the questionnaire for parents

Item	*Initial*	*Extraction*
Higher Education = good job security.	1.000	0.631
Education is the path to success at work.	1.000	0.447
Education protects humans against poverty.	1.000	0.446
Education is increasingly a guarantee of a higher income.	1.000	0.589
Education encourages entrepreneurial activity.	1.000	0.514
Highly educated people make up the nation's elite.	1.000	0.662
It is worthwhile to go abroad for a good education.	1.000	0.663
Schools are not required.	1.000	0.709
The main thing is a diploma.	1.000	0.627
Contacts are important.	1.000	0.535
Education in my country is a waste of time.	1.000	0.599
Being able to work is the most important thing.	1.000	0.607
One may make a good living without education.	1.000	0.548
Most people should have an education.	1.000	0.822
You cannot build a career without education.	1.000	0.605
Professionalism is more important than education.	1.000	0.532
Work will show up.	1.000	0.588
Education can be afforded only by those who have the money for it.	1.000	0.578
Graduation is required.	1.000	0.354
An educated person need not worry about not finding work.	1.000	0.537

Table 5.23 KMO and Bartlett's test of sphericity for the questionnaire for parents

Kaiser-Meyer-Olkin Measure of Sampling Adequacy		0.782
Bartlett's test of sphericity	Appor. chi-square	965.743
	df	190
	Sig.	0.000

questionnaire has good structural validity and meets the requirements for further factor analysis.

Table 5.24 shows that for the 20 core questions in this questionnaire, six factors are automatically extracted by the method of factor extraction of the principal component. The cumulative variance interpretation rate is 57.954%, and the total variance interpretation rate is greater than 50%. Overall, it shows that the exploratory factor result analysis is acceptable.

According to the score analysis of the "rotated component matrix", the items relating to each of the six factors are shown in Table 5.25.

On the basis of the items relating to each factor, and the investigation and survey of the educational concepts of parents and their educational

Table 5.24 Total variance of the parent questionnaire explained

Component	*Initial Eigenvalues*			*Extraction of Squared Loadings*			*Rotation Sums of Squared Loadings*
	Total	*% of Variance*	*Cumulative %*	*Total*	*% of Variance*	*Cumulative %*	*Total*
1	4.558	22.791	22.791	4.558	22.791	22.791	2.2.772
2	2.364	11.819	34.610	2.364	11.819	34.610	2.701
3	1.335	6.673	41.283	1.335	6.673	41.283	2.076
4	1.227	6.137	47.420	1.227	6.137	47.420	1.412
5	1.087	5.435	52.855	1.087	5.435	52.855	1.350
6	1.020	5.099	57.954	1.020	5.099	57.954	1.279
7	.942	4.708	62.662				
8	.867	4.334	66.998				
9	.829	4.144	66.996				
. . .							

viewpoints in this research, the following naming interpretation is performed for the six factors.

Factor 1: Education brings personal prosperity, social recognition and careers.
Factor 2: Education, especially abroad, is a guarantee of job security and financial security.
Factor 3: Education, a diploma and contacts are a guarantee of good work.
Factor 4: Education is not needed; professionalism and contacts are enough.
Factor 5: Education is a waste of time and for the rich; everyone can help themselves.
Factor 6: Education is good, but if there are contacts and professionalism, one's way of life can be good.

Results of the questionnaire

(1) MEAN, MEDIAN, MINIMUM, MAXIMUM AND STANDARD DEVIATION OF THE QUESTIONNAIRE

In the aforementioned statistics, for Q1, Q2, Q3, Q4, Q5, Q6, Q7, Q8, Q9, Q10, Q12, Q14, Q15 and Q16, the mean value is less than 3.00 and

Table 5.25 Items relating to each of the factors

	Item
Factor 1	Highly educated people make up the nation's elite.
	Education is increasingly a guarantee of a higher income.
	Education encourages entrepreneurial activity.
	It is worthwhile to go abroad for a good education.
	Education protects humans against poverty.
Factor 2	Education in my country is a waste of time.
	An educated person need not worry about not finding work.
	Education can be afforded only by those who have the money for it.
	Graduation is required.
	You cannot build a career without education.
	Work will show up.
Factor 3	The main thing is a diploma.
	Contacts are important.
	Education is the path to success at work.
	Higher Education = good job security.
Factor 4	Being able to work is the most important thing.
	Professionalism is more important than education.
Factor 5	Schools are not required.
	One may make a good living without education.
Factor 6	Most people should have an education.

the median is 2.00. This shows that more than 50% of the respondents accept these statements. For Q11 and Q18, the mean value is greater than 3.00 and the median is 4.00. This shows that more than 50% of the respondents do not accept these statements. For the remaining questions, Q13, Q17, Q19 and Q20, the median is 3. This shows that the percentage of the respondents choosing "I do not know" for these statements is less than 50%.

(2) SELECTED PHENOMENA WITH SIGNIFICANT FREQUENCY

Among the 20 core questions, those with higher frequencies are shown in Table 5.27.

According to the statistics, of the 20 questions, most of the parents agreed that "Education is the path to success at work" (86.7%), "Contacts are important" (80.3%) and "Most people should have an education" (82.7%). They mostly disagreed that "Education in my country is a waste of time" (56.1%) and "Education can be afforded only by those who have the money for it" (56.2%). The largest percentage of parents who gave the answer "I do not know" was for "Education is increasingly a guarantee of a higher income" (23.8%) and "You cannot build a career without education" (28.4%).

Table 5.26 Descriptive statistics main items measuring variance

Measuring Item	*N*		*Mean*	*Median*	*Minimum*	*Maximum*	*Std. Deviation*
	Valid	*Missing*					
Q1	210	1	2.12	2.00	1	5	0.661
Q2	210	1	1.82	2.00	1	5	1.009
Q3	210	1	2.22	2.00	1	5	0.569
Q4	210	1	2.38	2.00	1	5	0.493
Q5	207	4	1.99	2.00	1	5	1.006
Q6	208	3	2.21	2.00	1	5	0.615
Q7	208	3	2.42	2.00	1	5	0.419
Q8	207	4	2.58	2.00	1	5	0.424
Q9	208	3	2.05	2.00	1	5	0.865
Q10	208	3	1.92	2.00	1	5	1.269
Q11	207	4	3.50	4.00	1	5	–0.437
Q12	208	3	2.63	2.00	1	5	0.547
Q13	208	3	2.83	3.00	1	5	0.278
Q14	208	3	1.90	2.00	1	5	1.320
Q15	208	3	2.56	2.00	1	5	0.392
Q16	208	3	2.47	2.00	1	5	0.494
Q17	208	3	2.94	3.00	1	5	0.054
Q18	208	3	3.38	4.00	1	5	–0.368
Q19	208	3	2.86	3.00	1	5	0.188
Q20	208	3	3.11	3.00	1	5	–0.181

Table 5.27 The items with significant frequency

Statement	*Item*	*Frequency and Percentage*
Agree	Education is the path to success at work.	182 (86.7%)
	Contacts are important.	167 (80.3%)
	Most people should have an education.	172 (82.7%)
Disagree	Education in my country is a waste of time.	116 (56.1%)
	Education can be afforded only by those who have the money for it.	115 (56.2%)
I do not know	Education is increasingly a guarantee of a higher income.	50 (23.8%)
	You cannot build a career without education.	60 (28.4%)

(3) ITEMS RELATING TO BASIC ATTITUDES

There are three items relating to basic attitudes. The results can be described in terms of frequency.

I am satisfied with my child's education.

Among the parents who were surveyed, 81 parents strongly agree with the viewpoint "I am satisfied with my child's education", accounting for 38.4%

of the respondents; 78 agree with it, accounting for 37% of the respondents; 20 parents are uncertain about it, accounting for 9.5% of the respondents; 17 parents disagree with it, accounting for 8.1% of the respondents; 12 parents strongly disagree with it, accounting for 5.7% of the respondents (shown in Table 5.28). Three parents failed to give an answer.

I think the value of education is currently increasing.

Among the parents who were surveyed, 71 parents strongly agree with the viewpoint "I think the value of education is currently increasing", accounting for 33.6% of the respondents; 90 agree with it, accounting for 42.7% of the respondents; 30 parents are uncertain about it, accounting for 14.2% of the respondents; 11 parents disagree with it, accounting for 5.2% of the respondents; six parents strongly disagree with it, accounting for 2.8% of the respondents (shown in Table 5.29). Three parents failed to give an answer.

I wish my child to gain an education.

As shown in Table 5.31 among the parents who were surveyed, 130 parents strongly agree with the viewpoint "I wish my child to gain an education",

Table 5.28 Statistics for Item A on basic attitudes

	Frequency	*Percentage*	*Valid Percentage*	*Cumulative Percentage*
Valid SA	81	38.4	38.9	38.9
A	78	37.0	37.5	76.4
DK	20	9.5	9.6	86.1
D	17	8.1	8.2	94.2
SD	12	5.7	5.8	100.0
Total	208	98.6	100.0	
Answer missing	3	1.4		
Total	211	100.0		

Table 5.29 Statistics for Item B on basic attitudes

	Frequency	*Percentage*	*Valid Percentage*	*Cumulative Percentage*
Valid SA	71	33.6	34.1	34.1
A	90	42.7	43.3	77.4
DK	30	14.2	14.4	91.8
D	11	5.2	5.3	97.1
SD	6	2.8	2.9	100.0
Total	208	98.6	100.0	
Answer missing	3	1.4		
Total	211	100.0		

Table 5.30 Statistics for Item C on basic attitudes

	Frequency	*Percentage*	*Valid Percentage*	*Cumulative Percentage*
Valid SA	130	61.6	62.5	62.5
A	49	23.2	23.6	86.1
DK	14	6.6	6.7	92.8
D	7	3.3	3.4	96.2
SD	8	3.8	3.8	100.0
Total	208	98.6	100.0	
Answer missing	3	1.4		
Total	211	100.0		

accounting for 61.6% of the respondents; 49 agree with it, accounting for 23.2% of the respondents; 14 parents are uncertain about it, accounting for 6.6% of the respondents; seven parents disagree with it, accounting for 3.3% of the respondents; eight parents strongly disagree with it, accounting for 3.8% of the respondents. Three parents failed to give an answer.

(4) DEMOGRAPHIC DIFFERENCES AMONG THE PARENT QUESTIONNAIRE RESPONDENTS

Gender differences

In order to understand if there are differences in ideas about education between parents of different genders, the study uses the method of one-way ANOVA to examine it, the results of which are shown in Table 5.31.

The analysis of the differences shows that the *p*-value is greater than the level of significance, that is Sig>0.05. Therefore, there are no significant differences between parents of different genders in terms of their ideas about education.

Age differences

In order to understand if there are differences in ideas about education between parents of different ages, the study uses the method of one-way ANOVA to examine it, the results of which are shown in Table 5.32.

The analysis of the differences between parents in terms of their age shows that the factor "Education brings personal prosperity, social recognition and careers" is the one most affected by all the different factors so as to become a significant difference. However, there was no statistical significance with regard to the factors "Education, especially abroad, is a guarantee of security and financial security", "Education, a diploma, and contacts are a guarantee of good work", "Education is not needed; professionalism and contacts are enough", "Education is a waste of time and for the rich;

Table 5.31 The results of the ANOVA of parents by gender

		Sum of Squares	*df*	*Mean Square*	*F*	*Sig.*
REGR factor score 1 for analysis 1	Between Groups	1.403	1	1.403	1.406	.237
	Within Groups	201.597	202	0.988		
	Total	203.000	203			
REGR factor score 2 for analysis 1	Between Groups	1.607	1	1.607	1.612	.206
	Within Groups	201.393	202	0.997		
	Total	203.000	203			
REGR factor score 3 for analysis 1	Between Groups	0.024	1	0.024	0.024	.877
	Within Groups	202.976	202	1.005		
	Total	203.000	203			
REGR factor score 4 for analysis 1	Between Groups	1.505	1	1.505	1.508	.221
	Within Groups	201.495	202	0.998		
	Total	203.000	203			
REGR factor score 5 for analysis 1	Between Groups	0.673	1	0.673	.672	.413
	Within Groups	202.327	202	1.002		
	Total	203.000	203			
REGR factor score 6 for analysis 1	Between Groups	0.002	1	0.002	.002	.963
	Within Groups	202.998	202	1.005		
	Total	203.000	203			

Table 5.32 The results of the ANOVA of parents by age

		Sum of Squares	*df*	*Mean Square*	*F*	*Sig.*
REGR factor score 1 for analysis 1	Between Groups	26.515	26	1.020	1.023	.441
	Within Groups	176.485	177	0.997		
	Total	203.000	203			
REGR factor score 2 for analysis 1	Between Groups	39.509	26	1.520	1.645	.032
	Within Groups	163.491	177	0.924		
	Total	203.000	203			
REGR factor score 3 for analysis 1	Between Groups	26.012	26	1.000	1.001	.470
	Within Groups	176.988	177	1.000		
	Total	203.000	203			
REGR factor score 4 for analysis 1	Between Groups	27.506	26	1.058	1.067	.385
	Within Groups	175.494	177	0.991		
	Total	203.000	203			
REGR factor score 5 for analysis 1	Between Groups	22.489	26	0.865	.848	.680
	Within Groups	180.511	177	1.020		
	Total	203.000	203			
REGR factor score 6 for analysis 1	Between Groups	20.096	26	0.773	.748	.807
	Within Groups	182.904	177	1.033		
	Total	203.000	202			

everyone can help themselves" and "Education is good, but if there are contacts and professionalism, one's way of life can be good".

A further analysis was performed with a comparison of the means between groups. The factor "Education, especially abroad, is a guarantee of security and financial security" the main differences come from the viewpoints of the 19 parents who are more than 50 years old. Therefore, we have reasons to think that the result is disturbed by some individual data. There is no great difference between the viewpoints of the 192 parents who are 30 to 49 years old. Therefore, through the analysis of individual disturbance data, we may think that there is no significant statistical difference for parents of different ages with regard to this factor.

Differences in educational background

In order to understand if there are differences in the ideas about education between parents with different educational backgrounds, the study uses the method of one-way ANOVA to examine it, the results of which are shown in Table 5.33.

The analysis of the differences in the educational background of parents showed that the factor "Education, a diploma, and contacts are a guarantee of good work" is most affected by all the different factors so as to

Table 5.33 The results of the ANOVA of parents by educational background

		Sum of Squares	*df*	*Mean Square*	*F*	*Sig.*
REGR factor score 1 for analysis 1	Between Groups	8.174	4	2.044	2.087	0.084
	Within Groups	194.826	299	0.979		
	Total	203.00	203			
REGR factor score 2 for analysis 1	Between Groups	8.042	4	2.010	2.052	0.089
	Within Groups	194.958	199	0.980		
	Total	203.000	203			
REGR factor score 3 for analysis 1	Between Groups	10.341	4	2.585	2.670	0.033
	Within Groups	192.659	199	0.968		
	Total	203.000	203			
REGR factor score 4 for analysis 1	Between Groups	2.804	4	0.701	0.697	0.595
	Within Groups	200.196	199	1.006		
	Total	203.000	203			
REGR factor score 5 for analysis 1	Between Groups	4.078	4	1.202	1.020	0.398
	Within Groups	198.922	199	1.000		
	Total	203.000	203			
REGR factor score 6 for analysis 1	Between Groups	5.806	4	1.451	1.465	0.214
	Within Groups	197.194	199	0.991		
	Total	203.000	203			

become a significant difference. However, there was no statistical significance in the factors "Education brings personal prosperity, social recognition, and careers", "Education, especially abroad, is a guarantee of security and financial security", "Education is not needed; professionalism and contacts are enough", "Education is a waste of time and for the rich; everyone can help themselves" and "Education is good, but if there are contacts and professionalism, one's way of life can be good".

A further analysis was performed with a comparison of the means between groups. The factor "Education, a diploma, and contacts are a guarantee of good work" shows that those parents who did not receive an education attach importance to education and a diploma.

However, they attach even more importance to interpersonal relationships, as they think that finding a good job is often reliant on interpersonal relationships. In contrast, parents with a university educational background attach more importance to the education received by children. Although they also think that interpersonal relationships are very important in contemporary society, they think that educational background and the enhancement of ability are preconditions for being able to compete. Those parents with a lower secondary school educational background and upper secondary school educational background have basically the same viewpoints. They are between the parents with a high educational background and the parents with a background of illiteracy.

Results of the questionnaire survey for teachers

Questionnaires were distributed to teachers in lower secondary schools, upper secondary schools and special education schools in the selected regions mentioned earlier. The questionnaires were distributed and collected in person from July to November 2017. A total of 230 questionnaires were distributed and 230 were returned. Questionnaires with missing basic information and those suspected of plagiarism were excluded so that 214 valid questionnaires filled out by 214 teachers remained; 127 of them are teachers of lower and upper secondary schools, accounting for 59.3% of the total teacher sample; 87 of them are teachers of special education schools, accounting for 40.7%. What follows is the basic information about these teachers and their responses.

Basic situation of teachers in the questionnaire

Table 5.34 shows that, among the teachers surveyed in the questionnaire, 80 males accounted for 37.4% of the respondents; 134 females accounted for 62.6% of the respondents; the number of female teachers is considerably higher than that of male ones.

Table 5.34 Statistics for teachers' gender (*N* = 214)

Different Background Factors		*Sample Size (Person)*	*Percentage (%)*
(1) Gender of teachers			
Gender	Male	80	37.4
	Female	134	62.6

Table 5.35 Statistics for age of teachers (*N* = 214)

Different Background Factors		*Sample Size (Person)*	*Percentage (%)*
(2) Age status of teachers			
Age	20–29 years	99	46.3
	30–39 years	80	37.4
	40–49 years	32	15
	50 years and above	3	1.4

Table 5.35 shows that there are 99 teachers between the ages of 20 and 29, accounting for 46.3% of the respondents, 80 teachers between the ages of 30 and 39, accounting for 37.4% of the respondents, 32 teachers between the ages of 40 and 49, accounting for 15% of the respondents and three teachers above 50 years, accounting for 1.4% of the respondents. The largest number of teachers is in the 20–29 age group, and those aged over 50 are the smallest group.

Table 5.36 shows that there are 57 teachers with 0–3 years of professional experience, accounting for 26.6% of the respondents; 87 teachers have 4–10 years of professional experience, accounting for 40.7% of the respondents; 46 teachers have 11–19 years of professional experience, accounting for 21.5% of the respondents; 24 teachers have 20 years or more of professional experience, accounting for 11.2% of the respondents.

According to the statistics for the educational background of the teachers who were surveyed, there are two teachers with upper secondary school education, which accounts for 0.9% of the respondents; there are 42 teachers with a college degree, which accounts for 19.6% of the respondents; there are 163 teachers with a bachelor's degree, which accounts for 76.2% of the respondents; there are seven teachers with a master's degree, which accounts for 3.3% of the respondents. The largest number of teachers is educated to bachelor's degree level and the smallest number has upper secondary education (see Table 5.37).

(Higher education is further divided into two categories: (1) universities that offer four-year or five-year undergraduate degrees to award academic

Table 5.36 Statistics for length of professional experience of teachers (N = 214)

Different Background Factors		*Sample Size (Person)*	*Percentage (%)*
(3) Length of professional experience of teachers			
Length of professional experience	0–3 years	57	26.6
	4–10 years	87	40.7
	11–19 years	46	21.5
	20 years and above	24	11.2

Table 5.37 Statistics for the educational background of teachers (N = 214)

Different Background Factors		*Sample Size (Person)*	*Percentage (%)*
(4) Educational background of teachers			
Education	Upper secondary school	2	0.9
	College degree	42	19.6
	Bachelor's degree	163	76.2
	Master's degree	7	3.3

degree qualifications and (2) colleges that offer three-year diploma or certificate courses on both academic and vocational subjects.)

Reliability and validity analysis

(1) RELIABILITY ANALYSIS

The statistics for Cronbach's alpha are shown in Table 5.38.

According to the statistics for Cronbach's alpha of the questionnaire mentioned earlier, it is found that Cronbach's alpha is greater than 0.7, which indicates excellent validity of the questionnaire, which means that it meets the requirements of this research.

(2) VALIDITY ANALYSIS

Exploratory factor analysis is adopted to analyse the structural validity of the 20 core questions. The result shows that all the questions have a factor loading coefficient over 0.4. Thus, all of the 20 core questions are retained. The factor loading coefficients are analysed in Table 5.39.

Table 5.38 The statistics for Cronbach's alpha of the questionnaire for teachers

Cronbach's Alpha	*No. of Items*
0.804	25

Table 5.39 Cumulative analysis of the questionnaire for teachers

Item	*Initial*	*Extraction*
Higher Education = good job security.	1.000	0.529
Education is the path to success at work.	1.000	0.520
Education protects humans against poverty.	1.000	0.651
Education is increasingly a guarantee of a higher income.	1.000	0.576
Education encourages entrepreneurial activity.	1.000	0.673
Highly educated people make up the nation's elite.	1.000	0.437
It is worthwhile to go abroad for a good education.	1.000	0.530
Schools are not required.	1.000	0.673
The main thing is a diploma.	1.000	0.641
Contacts are important.	1.000	0.547
Education in my country is a waste of time.	1.000	0.635
Being able to work is the most important thing.	1.000	0.735
One may make a good living without education.	1.000	0.500
Most people should have an education.	1.000	0.546
You cannot build a career without education.	1.000	0.433
Professionalism is more important than education.	1.000	0.603
Work will show up.	1.000	0.516
Education can be afforded only by those who have the money for it.	1.000	0.640
Graduation is required.	1.000	0.591
An educated person need not worry about not finding work.	1.000	0.701

Table 5.40 KMO and Bartlett's test of the questionnaire for teachers

Kaiser-Meyer-Olkin Measure Adequacy		0.798
Bartlett's test of sphericity	Appor. chi-square	983.885
	df	190
	Sig.	0.000

Table 5.41 Total variance of the questionnaire for teachers explained (N = 214)

Component	*Initial Eigenvalues*			*Extraction of Squared Loadings*			*Rotation Sums of Squared Loadings*
	Total	*% of Variance*	*Cumulative %*	*Total*	*% of Variance*	*Cumulative %*	*Total*
1	4.254	21.272	21.272	4.254	21.272	21.272	2.992
2	2.498	12.492	33.764	2.498	12.492	33.764	2.569
3	1.661	8.305	42.069	1.661	8.305	42.069	1.699
4	1.168	5.840	47.909	1.168	5.840	47.909	1.597
5	1.132	5.661	53.571	1.132	5.661	53.571	1.549
6	.963	4.817	58.387	.963	4.817	58.387	1.271
7	.901	4.503	62.891				
8	.859	4.293	67.184				
9	.830	4.150	71.334				
. . .							

The 20 questions are analysed with exploratory factor analysis. Table 5.40 shows the KMO value of 0.798, much greater than 0.7. Bartlett's test of sphericity yields a P-value of 0.000. These data indicate that the questionnaire has good structural validity and meets the requirements for further factor analysis.

Table 5.41 shows that in this questionnaire, for the 20 core questions, six factors are automatically extracted by the method of factor extraction of the principal component. The cumulative variance interpretation rate is 58.387%, and the total variance interpretation rate is greater than 50%. Overall, it shows that the exploratory factor result analysis is acceptable.

According to the score analysis of the "rotated component matrix", the items relating to each of the six factors are shown in Table 5.42.

On the basis of the items relating to each factor, and the investigation and survey of the educational concepts of teachers and their educational viewpoint in this research, the following naming interpretation is performed for six factors.

Factor 1: Good education, especially abroad, is a guarantee of good work and employment.

Factor 2: Education is the foundation of social recognition and good work.

Table 5.42 Items relating to each of the factors

	Item
Factor 1	Education encourages entrepreneurial activity. Education protects humans against poverty. Education is increasingly a guarantee of a higher income. It is worthwhile to go abroad for a good education. Education is the path to success at work. Highly educated people make up the nation's elite.
Factor 2	An educated person need not worry about not finding work. Higher education = good job security. Work will show up. You cannot build a career without education. Graduation is required.
Factor 3	Education can be afforded only by those who have the money for it. One may make a good living without education. Education in my country is a waste of time.
Factor 4	Professionalism is more important than education. Most people should have an education.
Factor 5	Being able to work is the most important thing. Graduation is required.
Factor 6	Schools are not required. Contacts are important.

Factor 3: Education in our country is a waste of time and it is not necessary for one's career.

Factor 4: Education is socially important, but you can also build a career without it.

Factor 5: Education, especially abroad, is formally important, but contacts and hard work are decisive.

Factor 6: If the contacts and efforts are there, work will show up.

Results of the questionnaire

(1) MEAN, MEDIAN, MINIMUM, MAXIMUM AND STANDARD DEVIATION OF THE QUESTIONNAIRE

In the aforementioned statistics, for Q1, Q2, Q3, Q4, Q5, Q6, Q7, Q8, Q9, Q10, Q12, Q14 and Q16, the mean value is less than 3.00 and the median is 2.00. This shows that more than 50% of the respondents accept these statements. For Q11, Q18, Q19 and Q20, the mean value is greater than 3.00 and the median is 4.00. This shows that more than 50% of the respondents do not accept these statements. For the remaining questions, Q13, Q15 and Q17, the median is 3. This shows that the percentage of the respondents choosing "I do not know" is less than 50%.

(2) SELECTED PHENOMENA WITH SIGNIFICANT FREQUENCY

Among the 20 core questions, those with higher frequencies are shown in Table 5.44.

Table 5.43 Descriptive statistics for main items measuring variance

Measuring Item	*N*	*Mean*	*Median*	*Minimum*	*Maximum*	*Std. Deviation*
Q1	214	2.73	2.00	1	5	1.226
Q2	214	1.86	2.00	1	5	0.868
Q3	214	2.00	2.00	1	5	1.007
Q4	214	2.45	2.00	1	5	1.128
Q5	214	1.84	2.00	1	5	0.832
Q6	214	2.32	2.00	1	5	1.068
Q7	214	2.32	2.00	1	5	1.106
Q8	214	2.43	2.00	1	5	1.123
Q9	214	2.50	2.00	1	5	1.150
Q10	214	1.95	2.00	1	5	0.865
Q11	214	4.08	4.00	1	5	0.956
Q12	214	2.52	2.00	1	5	1.051
Q13	214	2.77	3.00	1	5	1.101
Q14	214	1.71	2.00	1	5	0.787
Q15	214	2.83	3.00	1	5	1.085
Q16	214	2.09	2.00	1	5	0.940
Q17	214	3.20	3.00	1	5	1.147
Q18	214	3.50	4.00	1	5	1.174
Q19	214	3.47	4.00	1	5	1.221
Q20	214	3.38	4.00	1	5	1.176

Table 5.44 The items with significant frequency

Statement	*Item*	*Frequency and Percentage*
Agree	Education is the path to success at work.	185 (86.4%)
	Education encourages entrepreneurial activity.	184 (86.0%)
	Most people should have an education.	192 (89.7%)
Disagree	Education in my country is a waste of time.	164 (76.6%)
	Education can be afforded only by those who have the money for it.	132 (51.7%)
	Graduation is required.	129 (60.3%)
I do not know	One may make a good living without education.	52 (24.3%)
	You cannot build a career without education.	50 (23.4%)

According to the statistics, out of the 20 questions, the largest numbers of teachers agreed that "Education is the path to success at work" (86.4%), "Education encourages entrepreneurial activity" (86%) and "Most people should have an education" (89.7%). The largest numbers disagreed that "Education in my country is a waste of time" (76.6%), "Education can be afforded only by those who have the money for it". (51.7%) and "Graduation is required" (60.3%). The largest percentage of teachers who gave the answer "I do not know" appeared for "One may make a good living without education" (24.3%) and "You cannot build a career without education" (23.4%).

(3) ITEMS CONCERNING BASIC ATTITUDES

There are five items that relate to basic attitudes. The results can be described in terms of frequency.

As shown in Table 5.45 among the teachers who were surveyed, 65 strongly agree with the viewpoint "I think the value of education is currently increasing", accounting for 30.4% of the respondents; 122 agree with it, accounting for 57% of the respondents; 22 are uncertain about it, accounting for 10.3% of the respondents; four disagree with it, accounting for 1.9% of the respondents; one teacher strongly disagrees with it, accounting for 0.5% of the respondents.

I think the knowledge and skills students are learning are what they need and expect.

Among the teachers who were surveyed, 43 strongly agree with the viewpoint "I think the knowledge and skills students are learning are what they need and expect", accounting for 20.1% of the respondents; 102 agree with it, accounting for 47.7% of the respondents; 39 are uncertain about it, accounting for 18.2% of the respondents; 24 disagree with it, accounting for 11.2% of the respondents; six teachers strongly disagree with it, accounting for 2.8% of the respondents (shown in Table 5.46).

Table 5.45 Statistics for Item A concerning basic attitudes

	Frequency	*Percent*	*Valid Percent*	*Cumulative Percent*
Valid SA	65	30.4	30.4	30.4
A	122	57.0	57.0	87.4
DK	22	10.3	10.3	97.7
D	4	1.9	1.9	99.5
SD	1	0.5	0.5	100.0
Total	214	100.0	100.0	

Table 5.46 Statistics for Item B concerning basic attitudes

	Frequency	*Percent*	*Valid Percent*	*Cumulative Percent*
Valid SA	43	20.1	20.1	20.1
A	102	47.7	47.7	67.8
DK	39	18.2	18.2	86.0
D	24	11.2	11.2	97.2
SD	6	2.8	2.8	100.0
Total	214	100.0		

Table 5.47 Statistics for Item C concerning basic attitudes

	Frequency	*Percent*	*Valid Percent*	*Cumulative Percent*
Valid SA	52	24.3	24.3	24.3
A	116	54.2	54.2	78.5
DK	30	14.0	14.0	92.5
D	15	7.0	7.0	99.5
SD	1	0.5	0.5	100.0
Total	214	100.0	100.0	

I think that the knowledge acquired by students at school will have a major impact on their future studies.

I think the value of education is currently increasing.

Among the teachers who were surveyed, 52 strongly agree with the viewpoint "I think that the knowledge acquired by students at school will have a major impact on their future studies", accounting for 24.3% of the respondents; 116 agree with it, accounting for 54.2% of the respondents; 30 are uncertain about it, accounting for 14% of the respondents; 15 disagree with it, accounting for 7% of the respondents; one teacher strongly disagrees with it, accounting for 0.5% of the respondents (see Table 5.47).

I think that the knowledge acquired by students at school will have a major impact on their future life.

As shown in Table 5.48 among the teachers who were surveyed, 58 strongly agree with the viewpoint "I think that the knowledge acquired by students at school will have a major impact on their future life", accounting for 27.1% of the respondents; 111 agree with it, accounting for 51.9% of the respondents; 28 are uncertain about it, accounting for 13.1% of the respondents; 16 disagree with it, accounting for 7.5% of the respondents; one teacher strongly disagrees with it, accounting for 0.5% of the respondents.

Table 5.48 Statistics for Item D concerning basic attitudes

	Frequency	*Percent*	*Valid Percent*	*Cumulative Percent*
Valid SA	58	27.1	27.1	27.1
A	111	51.9	51.7	79.0
DK	28	13.1	13.1	92.1
D	16	7.5	7.5	99.5
SD	1	0.5	0.5	100.0
Total	214	100.0	100.0	

Table 5.49 Statistics for Item E concerning basic attitudes

	Frequency	*Percent*	*Valid Percent*	*Cumulative Percent*
Valid SA	29	13.6	13.6	13.6
A	109	50.9	50.9	64.5
DK	34	15.9	15.9	80.4
D	35	16.4	16.4	96.7
SD	7	3.3	3.3	100.0
Total	214	100.0	100.0	

I am satisfied with students' education.
Among the teachers who were surveyed, 29 strongly agree with the viewpoint "I am satisfied with students' education", accounting for 23.6% of the respondents; 109 agree with it, accounting for 50.9% of the respondents; 34 are uncertain about it, accounting for 15.9% of the respondents; 35 disagree with it, accounting for 16.4% of the respondents; seven teachers strongly disagree with it, accounting for 3.3% of the respondents (shown in Table 5.49).

(4) DEMOGRAPHIC DIFFERENCES AMONG THE TEACHER QUESTIONNAIRE RESPONDENTS

Gender difference
In order to understand if there are differences in their ideas about education between teachers of different genders, the study uses the method of one-way ANOVA to examine it; the results are shown in Table 5.50.

The analysis of the differences shows that the *p*-value is greater than the level of significance, which is Sig > 0.05. Therefore, there are no significant differences between the ideas about education of the teachers who participated in the questionnaire that relate to their gender.

Table 5.50 The results of the ANOVA of the teachers by gender

		Sum of Squares	*df*	*Mean Square*	*F*	*Sig.*
REGR factor score 1 for analysis 1	Between Groups	.144	1	0.144	0.144	0.705
	Within Groups	212.856	212	1.004		
	Total	213.000	213			
REGR factor score 2 for analysis 1	Between Groups	1.102	1	1.102	1.102	0.295
	Within Groups	211.898	212	1.000		
	Total	213.000	213			
REGR factor score 3 for analysis 1	Between Groups	3.364	1	3.364	3.402	0.067
	Within Groups	209.636	212	0.989		
	Total	213.000	213			
REGR factor score 4 for analysis 1	Between Groups	0.011	1	0.011	0.011	0.918
	Within Groups	212.989	212	1.005		
	Total	213.000	213			
REGR factor score 5 for analysis 1	Between Groups	0.039	1	0.039	0.038	0.845
	Within Groups	212.961	212	1.005		
	Total	213.000	213			
REGR factor score 6 for analysis 1	Between Groups	2.366	1	2.366	2.382	.124
	Within Groups	210.634	212	.994		
	Total	213.000	213			

Table 5.51 The results of the ANOVA of the teachers by age

		Sum of Squares	*df*	*Mean Square*	*F*	*Sig.*
REGR factor score 1 for analysis 1	Between Groups	28.125	30	.938	0.928	0.579
	Within Groups	184.875	183	1.010		
	Total	213.000	213			
REGR factor score 2 for analysis 1	Between Groups	37.162	30	1.239	1.289	0.158
	Within Groups	175.838	183	0.961		
	Total	213.000	213			
REGR factor score 3 for analysis 1	Between Groups	26.476	30	0.883	0.866	0.670
	Within Groups	186.524	183	1.019		
	Total	213.000	213			
REGR factor score 4 for analysis 1	Between Groups	24.018	30	0.801	0.775	0.793
	Within Groups	188.982	183	1.033		
	Total	213.000	213			
REGR factor score 5 for analysis 1	Between Groups	39.611	30	1.320	1.394	0.097
	Within Groups	173.389	183	0.947		
	Total	213.00	213			
REGR factor score 6 for analysis 1	Between Groups	42.258	30	1.409	1.510	0.053
	Within Groups	170.742	183	0.933		
	Total	213.000	213			

Table 5.52 The results of the ANOVA of the teachers by educational background

		Sum of Squares	*df*	*Mean Square*	*F*	*Sig.*
REGR factor score 1 for analysis 1	Between Groups	2.278	3	0.759	0.757	0.520
	Within Groups	210.722	210	1.003		
	Total	213.000	213			
REGR factor score 2 for analysis 1	Between Groups	0.713	3	.238	0.235	0.872
	Within Groups	210.722	210	1.003		
	Total	213.00	213			
REGR factor score 3 for analysis 1	Between Groups	0.290	3	0.097	0.096	0.962
	Within Groups	212.710	210	1.013		
	Total	213.000	213			
REGR factor score 4 for analysis 1	Between Groups	2.211	3	0.737	0.734	0.533
	Within Groups	210.789	210	1.004		
	Total	213.000	213			
REGR factor score 5 for analysis 1	Between Groups	.237	3	0.079	0.078	0.972
	Within Groups	212.763	210	1.013		
	Total	213.000	213			
REGR factor score 6 for analysis 1	Between Groups	3.952	3	1.317	1.323	0.268
	Within Groups	209.048	210	0.995		
	Total	213.000	213			

Age difference

In order to understand if there are differences in their ideas about education between teachers of different ages, the study uses the method of one-way ANOVA to examine it; the results are shown in Table 5.51.

The analysis of the differences shows that the *p*-value is greater than the level of significance, which is Sig > 0.05. Therefore, there are no significant differences between the ideas about education of the teachers who participated in the questionnaire that relate to their age.

Differences in educational background

In order to understand if there are differences in the ideas about education between teachers with different educational backgrounds, the study uses the method of one-way ANOVA to examine it; the results are shown in Table 5.52.

The analysis of the differences shows that the *p*-value is greater than the level of significance, which is Sig > 0.05. Therefore, there are no significant differences between the ideas about education of the teachers who participated in the questionnaire that relate to their educational background.

Summary

Primarily, the questionnaire results are classified and presented by descriptive statistics, factor analysis, one-way ANOVA and other statistical approaches. The questions about core variables in the student, parent and teacher questionnaires are the same, while the questions that relate to basic attitudes differ. The respondents' answers to these same or different questions and selected results show the educational concept of the students, parents and teachers, as well as their educational viewpoint and attitude.

(1) On students

First, according to the statistical description in Table 5.9 and Table 5.10 for core variable question selection of the questionnaire, the students think that education is the path to occupational success and it can promote a business start-up. Therefore, the students think that most people should have an education. At the same time, they think that the promotion of professional skills is more important than the study of general knowledge. However, they do not think that only rich people can afford the cost of education. Moreover, they do not think education is a waste of time in China. They believe that there is an inextricable relationship between receiving education and finding a job. Therefore, we may assume that the students care about the role of education in their occupational development and care about whether education can promote their own ability.

Second, the questions about basic attitudes in the student questionnaire seek to ascertain the factors that influence the formation of the students' ideas about education. According to the answers, most of the students think that their parents have the greatest influence on their ideas about education, followed by the school. More than 50% of the students think that the media do not have a great influence on their ideas about education. This shows that the parents' ideas about education will directly influence the students' ideas about education and views on education. The degree of parents' attention to education will affect the development of education in the Tibetan regions.

Finally, according to the results of the analysis of the variance of demographic variables, in relation to the statements "Education is needed to get a good job" and "The level of education determines employment and careers", in the analysis of the variation between students of different genders, ages or types of schools, the *P*-value is less than the significance coefficient. This shows some influences of these fixed variables in this dimension. In contrast, the statements "A diploma from abroad and contacts are important for employment", "Education is needed but the ability to work and contacts are more important" and the other two dimensions are not affected by the different genders, ages and types of schools of the students. In other words, there is no difference in the statistical significance. We performed further analyses of variation in the responses to the questions, and we find that the type of school the students attend has certain effects on their ideas about and viewpoints of education, while the students' age and gender do not have obvious effects on their educational viewpoints.

(2) *On parents*

First, according to Table 5.26 and Table 5.27, which show the statistical results of the questionnaires, the parents think that education is the path to occupational success and most people should receive an education. Meanwhile, they think that a person can "go more smoothly" on the way to success if they obtain the opportunity to receive a good education. Moreover, the parents consider interpersonal relationships very important, and they attach great importance to a diploma and job opportunities. The parents disagree strongly with the statement that "education is a waste of time in China". Not a few parents feel that only rich people can afford the cost of education; however, more than 50% of the parents who were surveyed still disagree. Therefore, we may assume that the parents care about the social utilitarianism of education. They value the roles of education in the employment, income and quality of life of their children.

Second, the questions about basic attitudes in the parent questionnaire seek to ascertain the value of the parents' expectations with regard to their children's opportunity to receive an education and their degree of satisfaction with their children's education. According to the answers, more than 70% of the parents who were surveyed are satisfied with the education being received by their children. They also think that the value of education is constantly promoted at present, and they hope their children can obtain the opportunity to receive an education. Therefore, the parents are positive about education.

Finally, according to the results of the analysis of the variance of demographic variables, the parents' educational concepts and viewpoints are not affected by gender. In other words, there is no statistical significance of the differences between the different genders and the parents' educational concepts. Concerning the statements "Education, especially abroad, is a guarantee of security and financial security" and "Education, a diploma, and contacts are a guarantee of good work", the parents' responses are affected by their different ages or educational backgrounds. Four dimensions, including the statement "Education brings about human success and social recognition and occupational development", are not affected by the parents' different ages and educational backgrounds. According to the further analysis of the variance of each question, age and educational background only affect a few questions. Therefore, we think that the parents' gender, age and educational background do not have great effects on the formation of their educational concepts and their viewpoints and thoughts concerning education.

(3) *On teachers*

First, according to Table 5.43 and Table 5.44, the teachers who were surveyed also think that education is the path to occupational success and it can promote a person's ability to get started in business. Therefore, they believe most people should receive an education. The teachers also encourage the people who desire to obtain a higher-quality education to study abroad. They do not think that education in China is a waste of time. They do not think a diploma is more important than knowledge. They disagree that "Education can be afforded only by those who have the money for it"; however, the proportion of respondents who disagree with this statement is lower than those of students and parents. This shows that the teachers care about whether the students can enjoy a good education.

Second, the questions about basic attitudes in the teacher questionnaire seek to ascertain the teachers' degree of satisfaction with the current school education and their judgement of its educational value. According to the answers, the teachers' degree of agreement with the statement "The value of education is currently increasing" is not very high. However, they are relatively satisfied with the current school education. They think that the knowledge being learned by the students will have great effects on their studies and life in the future.

Finally, according to the analysis of the variance of the demographic variable, the statement "Education is the foundation of social recognition and good work" is slightly affected by differences in age. The response to "Education in our country is a waste of time and it is not necessary for a further career" is affected to some extent by the teachers' different educational backgrounds. Other responses are not affected by the differences in the teachers' gender, age and educational background, which shows that differences in gender, age and educational backgrounds do not have obvious effects on the formation of the teachers' educational concepts and opinions concerning education. In other words, there is no statistical significance difference between different genders, ages and educational backgrounds of the teachers and their educational concepts. According to the further analysis of the questions about differences, "different ages" only affects two among the 20 questions. "Different educational backgrounds" has only a slight effect on one question among the 20 questions. In the analysis of the significance of the differences, these can basically be ignored. Therefore, differences in the teachers' gender, age and educational backgrounds have no effects on the formation of their educational concepts and viewpoint and thoughts concerning education.

In short, the frequency of significance questions for students, teachers and parents is basically similar. They recognize the role of education in one's personal job, starting in business, and economic and other aspects. They think that education in China is not a waste of time and everyone should receive an education and have an opportunity to receive an education, as the basic education in China is free. However, the respondents ignore the relationship between the economy and the quality of education. Having an opportunity to receive education certainly does not mean enjoying the best education.

Results of interviews

Interviews are another common and effective method used in surveys (Wiersma & Jurs, 2010, p. 222). Semi-structured interviews were conducted with students, parents, teachers and monks to gain an understanding of their knowledge, opinions, expectations and satisfaction with school education in the Tibetan regions. The results can complement the study on the value orientation of education. This section presents background information about the interviewees and the interview results.

Results of the interviews with students

The students who were interviewed were recruited from general lower and upper secondary schools. As it was considered that disabled adolescents would not be able to handle deep communication, students from special education schools were not selected as interviewees. During the interviews, ten questions were asked concerning two dimensions: students' perception of their studies and their attitudes towards school education. The basic information about the interviewees and the responses to the remaining nine questions are provided later.

(1) Basic information about the interviewees

In this study, seven students were interviewed. In order to protect their personal privacy, the basic information about the interviewees includes only their gender, age and grade shown in Table 5.53.

(2) Interviewees' perception of their studies

The interviewees' perception of their studies is about the students' knowledge of subjects and their understanding of the function and meaning of

Table 5.53 Basic information about the students who were surveyed

Number	*Gender*	*Age*	*School (Grade)*
S1	Female	15	Lower secondary (2)
S2	Male	16	Lower secondary (2)
S3	Male	17	Upper secondary (2)
S4	Female	13	Lower secondary (2)
S5	Male	14	Lower secondary (1)
S6	Female	18	Upper secondary (2)
S7	Male	16	Upper secondary (2)

Note: The letter S in the number is the first letter of the word "student", and the order is the number of the interviewee.

studying. Their understanding of their current studies and level of thinking about them is ascertained through interviews with five questions. Their answers are summarized in the following text.

What subjects do you learn at school?

This question is asked to understand the subjects or what students need to learn at school.

Some of the interviewees said "Tibetan Language, Chinese Language, Geography, and History"; others listed "Tibetan Language, Chinese Language, Mathematics, English, History, Geography, Physics, Morality, Biology, Sports, and Music". Although there are differences in the curricula of lower secondary schools and upper secondary schools, two of the interviewees listed all the subjects and the other five students listed only some of the subjects.

Do you study the Tibetan language at school?

The Tibetan language is the mother tongue of the Tibetan people. It is the primary language used by Tibetan children in the vast agricultural and pastoral areas. However, the Tibetan language is considered an insignificant subject by many in Tibetan schools. Therefore, we specifically asked this question in the interviews. Of the seven interviewees, five students said that they studied the Tibetan language at school, while two students gave a different answer. We learn from the responses that not every Tibetan student is learning the Tibetan language, that is, some of the schools and classes in the Tibetan regions do not have Tibetan language as a subject.

What is your favourite subject and why?

When asked about their favourite subjects, most of the interviewees chose the Tibetan language, followed by English and politics. When asked why, the interviewees attributed the reasons to interest, humorous teachers and their improved communication skills and broadened horizons. These were the most popular reasons.

What is the subject you hate most and why?

Three of the students chose mathematics as the most unpopular subject; one chose geography; two chose English; one chose music. One of the students mentioned mathematics, English and history, and this was the only interviewee who chose more than one unpopular subject. They did not like the subjects because of poor grades, lack of interest and the teachers' strict requirements. Nearly half of the interviewees did not like mathematics. This is a problem worthy of attention, because we also found in the survey that many more upper secondary school students in the Tibetan regions choose to study liberal arts than sciences. This choice is most affected by the students' performance in mathematics.

What is your daily schedule? (Please provide your daily schedule at school and during the weekend or holidays)

Most of the interviewees provided their schedule in the morning, afternoon and evening at school. The answers show that both lower secondary school and upper secondary school students, whether resident or non-resident, basically wake up at 6 to 6:30 a.m. After breakfast, there will be a morning reading class before any formal class; there is a break after lunch, but many teachers will tutor the students during this break; the students usually have lunch and supper at school and spend one hour or so freely, before they start self-study at night. Non-resident students are dismissed at about 8 p.m., while resident students are dismissed at 9 p.m. Some of the interviewees said that they may go to bed later than 11 p.m. if they return home with extra homework. Only three out of the seven interviewees provided their weekend schedule. Over the weekend, they would play after finishing their homework. "We are so busy at school that we have no time to play. At weekends, all you want to do is have fun. But we still have so much homework to do and so many books to read, so there is little time to have fun", one interviewee said.

(3) Attitudes towards school education

This dimension is designed to gain an understanding of the students' satisfaction with, and expectations about, school education. There are five questions in total. The responses are summarized in the following text.

Do you think what you are learning now will benefit your future studies? Why?

All the interviewees believed that what they are learning now will benefit their future studies. Here are the main reasons they listed: (1) what they are learning now will be used in their future studies; (2) the more they learn now, the more they will know when they step into society and the less difficulty they will encounter at work; (3) there is much knowledge in society that is associated with our future; (4) what they are learning now will pave the way for their future studies; (5) there is always knowledge to learn wherever they go and (6) what they are learning now will help them know more.

Do you think what you are learning now will be helpful in your future life? Why?

All the interviewees believed that what they are learning now will be helpful in their future lives. Here are the reasons they gave: "I think knowledge is everywhere"; "Real life needs knowledge, and what we are learning now includes what we will need in our future lives"; "If we learn well now, life will be very easy in the future" and "What we are learning now is the source of knowledge in our future lives". They were sure of the future benefits of what they are learning now, although they did not explain how. That means they recognized the benefits of school education.

What do you most want to learn at school and why?

Three of the seven students answered that they most wanted to learn Tibetan history at school. "We would like to know the history and culture of our own people, but Tibetan history is hardly mentioned in the textbooks and the teachers do not tell us about it. We are very upset". Two students said that they were most eager to learn honesty. They said, "Honesty is fundamental to a human and his survival. It will be very important in our future life. However, learning the knowledge in books is regarded as the most important matter at school, while life guidance is neglected". One student expressed the desire to gain knowledge, because he thought "Knowledge will benefit our future life". This last student would like to learn as much as possible, especially gain more knowledge at school. These responses reflect the fact that the students not only expect to gain knowledge but also need guidance about their future life and social life from the school.

Do you think it is necessary to learn the Tibetan language and why?

Six of the interviewees thought that learning the Tibetan language is very necessary. They offered the following reasons: "We are Tibetans. We must learn the language of our own people and pass on our own culture". "It is not only the native language of our people, but also one of the important language tools that carry the fine culture of the Chinese nation". "Tibetan is my mother tongue and also an important language for me to learn in other courses". "As descendants of Tibetan nationality, we must learn the Tibetan language. It is unrealistic for us to rely on other nationalities to pass on our own language and texts". "Only when we study the Tibetan language can we help more Tibetans and teach more Tibetan children to learn the language as well". One interviewee said that it is unnecessary to learn the Tibetan language. "The Tibetan language is useless if we are admitted to a mainland school later. If we are not good at the Tibetan language, we can give up and spend the time learning other subjects". His answer actually represented the attitude of some of the children in the Tibetan regions towards their own language.

Are you happy at school? Why?

Six of the seven interviewees said that they had a good time at school. One student gave a different answer and explained that he was not good at the subjects taught at school, which made him stressed and unhappy. Those who felt happy provided the following reasons: "It is a happy thing for a minority child in a remote area to study at school". "The school can meet my needs". "I can not only gain knowledge at school, but also gain friendship and learn honesty, etc. School life is an important process in our life". "We feel happy because there are so many companions around us". "The teachers are strict, the classmates get along well, and I can gain knowledge very happily". "I have classmates around me and sometimes we chat with each other. Our relationships with our classmates and teachers develop. Not to mention that there are many kinds of books to read every day. As we read, we learn more and know more day by day. We are busy but happy every day". These varied reasons reflect the diversity of school life for the students.

Results of the interviews with parents

The parent interviewees were recruited from the respondents to the questionnaire. They are parents of students from both general and special education secondary schools at lower and upper levels. The interview included seven questions dealing with two dimensions: the parents' knowledge of their child's studies at school and their attitude towards school education. The basic information about the parents who were interviewed and their answers to the seven questions are provided in Table 5.54.

Table 5.54 Basic information about the parents who were surveyed

(1) Basic information about the interviewees

Number	*Gender*	*Age*	*Education*	*School (Child)*
P1	Male		University	Lower secondary school
P2	Male		Technical secondary	Lower secondary school
P3	Male		Primary	Lower secondary school
P4	Female		College	Upper secondary school
P5	Male		Illiterate	Special education school
P6	Female		Technical secondary	Special education school
P7	Female		Upper secondary	Special education school

Note: The letter P in the number is the first letter of the word "parent", and the numbering is the number of the interviewee.

(2) Knowledge of their child's studies

The parents' knowledge of their child's studies was reflected in their familiarity with, and care for, their child's education. Three questions were included. The feedback on the interviews is presented in the following.

Do you know what subjects your child learns at school?

Four of the parents who were interviewed said that they knew what subjects their child learned at school, while three said that they were not sure. The negative group was understandable, because the three parents were illiterate or had dropped out at the elementary school level. They were not even clear about all of the subjects. When asked to list the subjects during the interview, four parents just mentioned the Chinese language, Tibetan language, mathematics, history and sports. It can be concluded that most of the interviewees are not very clear about what their child learns at school and that they are not deeply involved in their child's studies.

What is your child's favourite subject and why?

Two of the parents said that their child likes history. "As citizens of the People's Republic of China, the kids need to understand the long history and culture of the country". "Because there are many stories in the history class, my child has liked to listen to stories since his childhood. No doubt he is particularly interested in history". Two of the parents said that their child likes Tibetan Language because "The Tibetan language is their mother tongue and it's easy to understand". These four interviewees were parents of general school students. Two parents of students from special education schools said that their child likes Tangka painting and massage classes, because they think this knowledge will benefit their future life. One parent replied that his child does not like any subject in particular.

Does your child learn the Tibetan language at school?

Four of the interviewees answered that their child learns the Tibetan language at school; three said that their child does not learn it. Two of the interviewees who gave a negative answer were parents of students from special education schools. It can be concluded that the absence of a Tibetan language class is more common in special education schools than in general schools.

(3) Attitudes towards school education

The interview in this dimension is designed to gain an understanding of parents' willingness to send their child to school, their expectations about their child's learning and their satisfaction with school education. There are four questions in the interview.

Are you willing to send your child to school? Why?

All seven parents who were interviewed said that they are willing to send their child to school. Here are the reasons given by the parents of general school students: "Receiving a school education can change his fate". "I send him to school because he will have the opportunity to go to college and won't end up as a farmer". "A school education allows him to have a greater chance of finding a job in a government office or institution, and life will not be that hard for him". "At school, the kid can learn cultural knowledge and will have a better life when he steps into society in the future". The parents of students from special education schools provided the following reasons for their willingness to send their child to school. "We don't have to pay for the tuition. The teachers not only teach the children cultural knowledge but also take care of their life patiently. So I have no worries at all". "At school, the children can learn sewing, massage, and other skills. I think that these skills will help him become a breadwinner in the future". It is clear that the parents are willing to send their child to school because they believe a school education will lead the child to a good life in the future. However, the parents of general school students and those of special education school students have somewhat different expectations about school education and their child's future social life.

Do you think children need to learn the Tibetan language at school? Why?

All seven parents who were interviewed agreed that children need to learn the Tibetan language at school. They offered the following reasons: "As Tibetans, our children must first learn the Tibetan language before they learn other languages". "We must learn and use the Tibetan language. It is unrealistic to rely on other nationalities to pass on our own language and texts". "The children need to learn the Tibetan language because this is our own language". "As Tibetan people, if we give up our own culture, do we still have our dignity?" "Learning the language of our own nation is a matter of course. If the descendants of a nation do not learn their language, the nation may die out some day". The parents' answers show their strong sense of national responsibility, but it is surprising that they do not mention what the Tibetan language means to the future life and career of their child or to their adaptability to society.

What do you think the children need to learn most at school and why?

Two of the parents who were interviewed said that the children most need to learn the Tibetan language at school. They listed the following reasons: "Children should learn the Tibetan language from an early age since it is the language of their nation". "My child will return to the Tibetan region after completing his studies at school. Although you don't have to learn the Tibetan language just because you live in the Tibetan region, it will become an indispensable part of your life and work". One parent said in the interview that the children should learn both the Tibetan language and the Chinese language at school because "as minority members, they need to know both the language of their nation and the mainstream language of their country, so that they can find a job more easily". One interviewee answered that the children should learn the Chinese language well because "The Chinese language is more useful in the workplace and in the community". One parent said that he wanted his child to learn various types of knowledge at school because he "expect(ed) his child to become a fully-developed person". Two other parents of students from special schools thought that learning the ability to take care of themselves at school is the most important type of knowledge for the children.

Are you satisfied with the school education and why?

Five of the parents who were interviewed said that they are satisfied with the school education. Their reasons include: "The teachers are all responsible". "The teachers try to use the Tibetan language in class, and the children can understand what they say more easily". "Although we live in a poor and remote ethnic area, the state and the government have invested substantial funds in creating sound conditions for the children to pursue their studies". "The children not only learn cultural knowledge, but also develop the ability to take care of themselves". "My child now cares more about us and is becoming more respectful and more polite than before. It happened after he entered the school. I am very satisfied". Two of the parents said that they are not satisfied with the school because "There is no Tibetan language class at school" and "The school focuses only on all kinds of examinations and pays no attention to the development of students' skills and conduct". In short, most of the parents are satisfied with the schools.

Results of the interviews with teachers

The teachers who were interviewed were recruited from those teachers at general schools and special education schools who participated in the questionnaire survey. The interview included seven questions dealing with two dimensions: their perception of students' learning at school and attitude towards school education (as shown in Table 5.55).

(1) Basic information about the interviewees

(2) Perception of students' learning

Two questions are designed to ascertain what the teachers know about the knowledge and skills the students are learning.

Do you think the students are learning the knowledge and skills they need? Why?

Four of the interviewees said that the students are learning the knowledge and skills they need. They gave the following reasons: "The courses offered at school are both comprehensive and suitable for the target age groups of the students. They also cover various knowledge and skills. As Tibetan children, it would be better if they could learn the knowledge in their native language. Teaching classes in their mother tongue could be of great help to the children in the Tibetan regions, especially in pastoral regions". "The design of the school curriculum fully allows for the knowledge and skills that the students need". "English, the subject I teach, is what the students need if they want to go global and understand the wider world". "Our educational goal is to cultivate talents that will contribute to society, so the knowledge and skills the students learn are exactly what is needed to put this goal into practice". Three interviewees believed that the knowledge and skills the students learn at school are hardly what they need. They said that "What the students need should be future-oriented, but no one knows what knowledge and skills will be needed in the future". "The school education now only focuses on improving the scores and dealing

Table 5.55 Basic information about the teachers who were surveyed

Number	*Gender*	*Age*	*education*	*Subject Taught*	*School*
T1	Male	50	College	Tibetan	Lower secondary school
T2	Male	24	University	Tibetan	Lower secondary school
T3	Female	36	University	Maths	Lower secondary school
T4	Male	48	College	Tibetan	Special education school
T5	Female	25	University	Rehabilitation	Special education school
T6	Male	52	University	Physical education	Upper secondary school
T7	Male	40	University	English	Upper secondary school

Note: The letter T in the number is the first letter of the word "teacher", and the numbering is the number of the interviewee.

with exams. It pays little attention to the students' needs and ignores the nature of education, that is, promoting students' all-round development". "Students have the right and obligation to receive education, but it seems that they don't have the right to choose what kind of education to receive. So it is difficult to determine whether the students are learning what they need". It can be seen that more than half of the interviewees believed that the students are learning what they need, while nearly half of them were not sure about that.

Do you think the students are learning the knowledge and skills they expect? Why?

Five of the interviewees said that the students are not necessarily learning the knowledge and skills that they expect. They believed so for the following reasons: "The students are too young to be sure about their learning expectations, and their expectations may be changeable and not well controlled. The decisions are usually made by parents and teachers". "Students at their age seldom have well-grounded expectations". "I think the students' expectations about knowledge and skills are temporary, and the small knowledge and skills they are learning now will not live up to their ultimate expectations". "Actually, what they expect is learning while playing". "There is a gap between what the students are learning and what they expect, because there is a gap between their knowledge and their life". Two of the interviewees believed that the students are learning the knowledge and skills that they expect. Their reasons were as follows: "Getting good grades in different subjects is what they expect". "They come to school in the expectation of acquiring knowledge and skills in different subjects. This is exactly what they are doing right now". The answers suggested that the teachers were not very satisfied with what is taught at school.

(3) Attitudes towards school education

There are four questions in this dimension. They are designed to ascertain how the teachers evaluate the influence of school education on the future studies and life of the students and their satisfaction with school education.

Do you think the students need to learn the Tibetan language, and why?

Six of the teachers who were interviewed said that the students need to learn the Tibetan language at school. They thought that "Learning the Tibetan language is really important for a school in a region inhabited by a minority or for a minority school, because it is their first language. It would be difficult for the students to accept another language, and their studies will be negatively affected". "Learning the Tibetan language is necessary because we need to pass on the traditional Tibetan culture". "The Tibetan language is very practical in this region inhabited by a minority; it is very necessary to learn it. For any ethnic group, individual development must be built on the learning of their native language". One interviewee believed that the students do not necessarily need to learn the Tibetan language. "It is not necessary for students to learn the Tibetan language, except those in the Tibetan regions and places where the Tibetan language is used. I mean that students should not be required to learn the Tibetan language if they do not live in the Tibetan regions or in places where the Tibetan language is used. Since they will not use it in life or at work, there is no need to waste time learning it".

Do you think what the students learn at school will greatly influence their future studies? Why?

Five of the interviewees said that what the students learn at school would greatly influence their future studies. They explained the reasons as follows: "The knowledge they now learn in the school is an important basis for all the cultural knowledge they need to learn in their life". "The knowledge taught at school is basic and practical. For example, I teach English and it is very practical in social activities". "Knowledge can change one's fate". These interviewees emphasized the role of knowledge in the students' future. Another two interviewees did not agree. Their reasons were as follows: "No one is sure about what they are going to learn in the future, but they must study hard at school". "The knowledge taught at school is so limited that high grades do not necessarily guarantee a good future". It seems that most of the interviewees felt that the future is so uncertain and broad that no one could be sure about how it will be influenced by the knowledge being taught now.

Do you think what the students learn at school will greatly influence their future life? Why?

A total of five interviewees believed that what the students learn at school would greatly influence their future life. They explained their answer in the following way. "For most students, academic performance at school spells their fate". "If students gain more knowledge at school, even if they might not have a glorious future, they can live better. In contrast, students who gain little or even no knowledge at school may end up in dishonest practices or even crimes in the future". "The knowledge that students gain at school may determine their future fate". "The knowledge that students now gain at school can be useful in their future lives and thus benefit their future". "Knowledge can enhance students' abilities in all aspects and has a role to play in students' future lives. It is a necessity of life itself". They were strongly convinced that what is taught at school can change the students' future. Two interviewees said that what the students learn at school will not have much influence on their future life. One of them explained that "Many students learn from books, and their abilities are not tested. This is an educational problem. The knowledge that students keep in mind at school will no longer be useful in society. So I think school education will not lead students anywhere". "The students are learning nothing more than basic and simple knowledge from textbooks, but their future life will be colourful, so there is little influence we are talking about here". Some interviewees thought that what is taught at school is simple and limited, as it is exam oriented. They claimed that there is a lack of teaching and training of skills and that the knowledge the students gain now will not greatly influence their future colourful life.

Are you satisfied with the school education and why?

Three interviewees were satisfied with the school education for the following reasons: "There is a complete internal system and a good working environment at school". "There is a good environment for teaching and educating people at school, and the students are immersed in a strong learning atmosphere". "I can accept the school administrators' management philosophy and methods, as well as the teaching modes applied here". They were satisfied with the working environment at school and the learning atmosphere for students. One interviewee said that he was basically satisfied because "The school does not make adequate efforts to build the teaching staff and the students do not perform satisfactorily in unified examinations. And there are many other problems, but the school insists on a good overall direction after all". While he realized there are many problems to be solved, he thought that the school is developing well as a whole. Another interviewee provided a mixed answer. "I am satisfied with the teaching of basic knowledge, but I don't think we do a good job in training students' abilities. The school only pays attention to the former and ignores the latter", he said. He tried to analyse the pros and cons of school education with an objective attitude. Two of the interviewees confessed that they were not satisfied with the school education. One reason was that "The teachers are burdened with a heavy teaching load", while the other reason was that "There are few opportunities to learn Tibetan culture at school. A course about the national traditional culture should be properly included in the curriculum of the school, such as Tangka painting, basic Buddhist theory, Hetuvidya (science of causes in Buddhist logico-epistemology), and Sanskrit. After all, education has to perform the function of passing on cultural heritage". They expressed their satisfaction with school education with regard to whether the division of labour among the teachers was reasonable and the cultural inheritance function of education sum ca pawas performed.

Results of the interviews with monks

Monks are the recipients of Tibetan traditional education. Their understanding of monastic education and their attitude towards school education will be insightful for this study. The information will form the cultural foundation on which to further analyse the value orientation of education and interventions in special education for disabled adolescents. The monks were interviewed with regard to two dimensions: "awareness of their own learning" and "attitude towards monastic education and school education". The basic personal information and interview responses of the monks are described in Table 5.56.

(1) Basic information about the interviewees

(2) Awareness of their own learning

Three questions are designed to learn about the way of learning, the content of the studies and the daily schedule in the monastery so as to catch a glimpse of traditional Tibetan education.

Can you briefly describe what you mostly learn?

All the seven monks who were interviewed said that they mainly learn "knowledge of Buddhism", but they offered different definitions of such knowledge. For example, some said that the Buddhist knowledge they learn is "scripture readings that promise them happiness in the afterlife and esoteric Buddhism". Some said, "The knowledge of Buddhism is one

Table 5.56 Basic information about the monks who were surveyed

Number	*Gender*	*Age*	*Length of Learning*
M1	Male	25	7
M2	Male	19	2
M3	Male	24	6
M4	Male	40	26

Note: The letter M in the number is the first letter of the word Monk, and the numbering is the number of the interviewees.

based on Hetuvidya, as Guru Dignāga puts it; 'Hetuvidya is a mirror of any subject knowledge that is needed in the future' ". Others said, "It is a collection of various esoteric teachings and knowledge of axiology". One interviewee revealed that they have to learn different subjects and knowledge including Sum cu pa (grammatical work by Thonmi Sambhota, the inventor of the Tibetan script), Tibetan grammar and Tibetan phonology, poetry, rhythm and history in addition to the knowledge of Buddhism.

What is your daily schedule?

Three of the monks who were interviewed said that they do not have a regular daily schedule. They usually read and recite scriptures after getting up. After breakfast, they attend class or, when there is no class, they study in the dormitory or participate in scripture debate training. The scripture debate is a way of learning. Two or more are trained in the form of debate to understand and consolidate their knowledge of Buddhism. One interviewee said that he gets up at 7 a.m. and goes to bed at 11 p.m. Specifically, he recites the essential knowledge of various subjects after getting up at 7 a.m., has breakfast from 8 a.m. to 9 a.m., attends the class of scripture teachers from 9:00 to 10:30, finishes the chanting mission for the worship of pilgrims from 10:30 to 11 a.m. and attends the temple-wide scripture lecture of a master from 11 a.m. to 12 noon. Next, he has lunch from 12 noon to 1 p.m., takes a break from 1 to 2 p.m., studies in the dormitory from 2 to 3 p.m., reviews what he learned in the morning under the tutorship of a scripture teacher from 3:30 to 4 p.m., starts debate training with a partner from 4 to 6:30 p.m. and has supper from 6 to 7:30 p.m. After supper, he attends the lecture of a scripture teacher from 7:30 to 9 p.m., has a review session in the dormitory from 9 to 10:30 p.m. and usually goes to bed at 11 p.m.

What is your biggest change after receiving a temple education and why?

Four of the interviewees said that they become altruistic and are always ready to help others after receiving a temple education. They also indicated that they have abandoned material desires and a utilitarian attitude. These are the positive changes they mentioned, but they also talked about certain negative ones. For example, some interviewees said, "I feel that I have become a bit superstitious and not determined enough". Some also confessed that they are more paranoid about the teachings of the Buddha and so single-minded that they refuse to think too much. These answers are pertinent, suggesting both positive and negative changes.

(3) Attitude towards a monastic education and school education

Three questions are designed to understand how the monks see and evaluate a monastic education and a school education.

What do you think is the biggest advantage of a monastic education and why?

One interviewee said, "I think the greatest merit of a monastic education is that it advocates altruism and the pursuit of spiritual well-being. The ultimate result of the study of Buddha is the development of an altruistic mind. The pursuit of inner happiness is hindered by five annoyances: greed, hatred, ignorance, arrogance, and jealousy. The only way to get rid of these five annoyances is to study Buddhism, which is also the only way to pursue happiness in life". Another interviewee said, "I think the biggest merit of a monastic education is that it instructs people to cultivate their minds. The way to do so is integrating oneself into the law, guiding all beings to the right track of a happy life, and treating all sentient beings without bias". The other interviewees believed that "A monastic education is good as it educates people, regardless of their abilities and financial resources, always to be altruistic. It also emphasizes that everyone who studies in a monastery should have his own specialization or focus on his strength to learn a certain skill". The core idea of Buddhism is to work for the good of sentient beings with compassion and kindness. Their answers disclosed that monastic education focuses on both the spiritual and physical cultivation of people.

What do you think is the biggest shortcoming of a monastic education and why?

One interviewee said, "The study of Buddha emphasizes listening, contemplation, and reflection, but now these three approaches are disconnected in a monastic education. That's why the purpose of spiritual and physical upbringing is not well achieved". Another interviewee explained that "The monastic education in the Tibetan regions is too focused on the Buddha's teachings and excludes other thoughts. It overemphasizes the philosophy of unworldliness while neglecting the opposite". One interviewee said, "A monastic education does not regard this life as the main goal, so it does not play a due role in the construction of social culture and fails to reform with the times. It also mainly relies on traditional teaching styles that do not arouse the interest of learners. The teaching content does not fit in with the habits of modern people". The interviewees talked about the drawback of a monastic education in engagement with society. Perhaps it can be understood as a shortcoming in the teaching and practice of productive labour skills.

What do you think about school education and why do you think so?

Regarding school education, one interviewee said that he did not have an in-depth understanding of school education; however, he shared some views based on his experience. "School education encourages different thinking and keeps up with the times. Students who have received a school education show stronger creativity. This is a good side of school education. But a coin has two sides. For example, school education tends to overemphasize results, and students easily become competitors", he said. According to another interviewee, "The pursuit of immediate interests and the fame and fortune of this life should not be the values of school education. Measuring everything by money should not be a value orientation, either. However, such utilitarian values are somehow popular in school education, and as a result many selfish egoists are trained. Material desires outweigh spiritual pursuit, which renders students prone to psychological problems. They are happy when they get what they want; they are sad when their needs are not met. They are too fragile to withstand failures and setbacks. This trend can be detected from the increasing news reports about student suicides, thefts, and robbery in society. So I suggest that schools should pursue positive education that encourages kindness and altruism". Another interviewee believed that "The biggest problem with school education in Tibetan regions is that the Tibetan language and culture are not given due respect and attention. At most public schools, students are deprived of the opportunity to learn about their own culture. School leaders, local leaders, and government authorities rob children of the right and need to learn the Tibetan language for the sake of social development. It is also worth noting that now schools teach nothing but textbooks and neglect ideological and moral education in order to send students to colleges and help them find a job. Driven by this goal, many graduates care for personal enjoyment only and refuse to contribute to society, people, or the development of the nation, although they do enter university and find a job. Of course, there are more and more opportunities for learning Tibetan culture at private schools and some public ones. This shows that school education is also constantly developing". These answers represent objective criticism of the utilitarianism and pragmatism of school education.

Summary

Although the interviewees were asked different questions, the aim of all questions was to understand the interviewees' perception of students' learning and their basic attitudes towards school education. Therefore, the results of the interviews with regard to these two dimensions can be summarized as follows.

(1) Perception of students' learning

This dimension was first and foremost focused on the perception of what the students learn at school. Parents and students were required to list the subjects taught at school. Most of the parents who were interviewed said that they were clear about the subjects that their child needs to learn at school. However, further communication showed that more than half of the parents were not sure about what specifically their child was learning. The students did not list all the subjects, either. This suggests that they simply listed the subjects that are valued at school or that they are interested in. The teachers were asked in a different way to evaluate whether what the students learn meets their needs and expectations. In this regard, most of the teachers were not very sure whether the students are learning what they need and expect. They claimed that students of this age are not able to know what knowledge they need except for following the instructions of their school, teachers, and parents. What is more, their expectations are changing constantly. These answers suggested that teachers and students at Tibetan schools do not communicate about the content of learning and its selection. The teachers strictly follow the textbooks prescribed by the state, and the students follow the teachers' instructions obediently. They do not question the reasonableness of the determined learning content.

In addition, as regards whether the Tibetan language is taught at school, not every school in the Tibetan regions provides Tibetan language classes and not every class learns the Tibetan language. However, the Tibetan language was the most popular subject among the students and also among the parents when they listed their child's favourite subject. They explained that from a subjective perspective, learning the Tibetan language is not only their duty as Tibetans, but it is also their native language, which can be understood and learned easily. The students who chose a favourite subject other than the Tibetan language attributed their reasons to the teaching methods and requirements of teachers. This indicated that the approach of the teachers can greatly influence the academic development of students.

Finally, with respect to the daily schedule of students, they spend more than 10 hours at school every day. When the self-study classes in the morning and evening are included, the students have more than 10 class hours per day. This is a heavy learning schedule for the students at lower secondary schools and upper secondary schools in the Tibetan regions. They have little free time.

We have a basic idea of the current state of school education in the Tibetan regions from the interviews in this dimension. We realize that school education in the Tibetan regions needs to strengthen the teaching of the Tibetan language and provide students with the opportunity to learn about Tibetan history and culture. What needs to be done most is to improve the students' wisdom in creating a happy life in the future.

(2) Basic attitudes towards school education

First of all, when asked whether what they learn would influence their future studies and life, all the students who were interviewed gave a positive answer. They thought that there must be a connection between the knowledge they learn today and the knowledge they will learn some day in the future. Their future studies will be easier for them if they lay good foundations now. Some also believed that how much they learn now will influence the quality of their future studies and life, because knowledge can change people's destiny. It can be seen that the students have a blind belief in knowledge and they tend to believe that the knowledge taught at school will surely be useful for their future studies and life. This result reflects the fact that school education in Tibetan regions focuses on the instillation of knowledge while neglecting the development of critical thinking in students. In this respect, the parents shared almost the same understanding as the students. Almost all of them considered that what their child learns now would influence their future studies and life. In fact, these responses simply confirm the finding of our previous survey in the Tibetan regions that parents are rarely involved in school education. However, the teachers shared more thoughts on this question. Some teachers thought that school education pays attention to exams and teaches students exam-taking knowledge and ability more than other skills. They thus concluded that what the students learn now would not necessarily influence their future studies and life greatly.

Second, when asked whether students need to learn the Tibetan language, all the interviewees provided a positive answer. This was the only one unified and resolute answer among all of the respondents during all of the interviews. Two of the reasons they provided merit attention. For one thing, the Tibetan language is the native language of the vast majority of the students, while the Chinese language is used in the classes of different subjects. Students have difficulty in learning the subjects well because of the language barrier. This is the most important reason why the quality of education in minority areas has not been improved for a long time. For another, the cultural continuity of a nationality depends on its language. As future inheritors and passers-on of the national culture, the students will not be able to shoulder the important burden if they do not learn their native language. A thought-provoking issue is that although most of the students will still return to the Tibetan regions and live in the Tibetan communities, almost none of the interviewees talked about the role of the Tibetan language in their future life.

Furthermore, all of the students except one said that they have a good time at school, and five of the parents and four of the teachers said they were satisfied with the school education. The results show that parents and students in the Tibetan regions trust schools and most of the teachers recognize the merits of schools. However, a preliminary analysis of the reasons for their happiness and satisfaction shows that their positive comments result from the hardware conditions and equipment of the schools, the teachers' sense of responsibility and the benefits of friendship and good faith. Few of them mentioned how the school education would benefit the future studies and life of the students. A few respondents who were dissatisfied with school education explained that schools overemphasize exam-oriented education and neglect the improvement of quality and the development of various abilities in students. They also mentioned that schools in minority areas fail to provide students with opportunities to learn cultural knowledge about their nationality and do not offer courses that adapt to local life or productive labour.

Finally, monks who receive a traditional Tibetan monastic education were interviewed in this study. They shared their detailed understanding of the monastic education they receive, which has been elaborated on earlier. They had mixed responses when asked about their opinion on school education. They acknowledged the way in which schools train multicultural quality and diverse thinking in students. However, they were worried about the fact that schools pay disproportionate attention to teaching knowledge while neglecting the development of students' abilities and a sound personality. They also believed that education should empower students to pursue a happy life.

In short, the interviews with different respondents found the answers to the two questions raised in this study: What is the value of Tibetan traditional culture? Is the value orientation of school education influenced by the traditional cultural values of Tibetans? The interview results also confirm the hypothesis that the value orientation of school education is positively related to the value orientation of Tibetan culture.

A case study: principal of a school for blind children in Tibet

One of the researchers tried to find some cases but in vain. It was very frustrating. As he browsed the boring updates in the friends' circle of WeChat, he accidentally saw a post from one of his students who worked at a TV station. It was about her interview with a man who is the blind principal of a school for blind children. After watching this 25-minute interview several times as if it were a treasure, the researcher asked the student to find the principal for further contact. The principal of the school was willing to collaborate.

A few days later, the researcher met the principal in a hotel in Chengdu. He was a very warm and talkative person. Some basic information about him is as follows.

The principal was born in GZ County, Sichuan Province, in 1988. He lost his sight at the age of 3 and came to the city of Lhasa with his mother at the age of 14. He entered a school for blind children in Lhasa, where he spent his early school years. The education of the school for blind children focuses on inspiring intelligence, especially the hands-on ability and various talents of children. Naturally intelligent, he soon stood out and became a key student at the school. In 2005, when he had been studying at the school for three years, he was sent to study English in London, England. After returning home, he became a member of the management of the school. In 2009, he became the principal, whom more than 20 children at the school relied on. In 2014, he married a beautiful girl who was working at the school. They were the first couple in the school. The birth of a healthy and lovely baby girl in the following year made them a happy family of three.

In recent years, he has been invited to give lectures at Tsinghua University, Peking University and Hong Kong University. He has studied and travelled in the United States, India, Germany, South Korea and many other countries. These experiences have not only enriched his life but also given him a chance to share his self-confidence, optimism and positive attitude to life with every audience. His life story has enabled more people to truly understand and appreciate the blind and has inspired many ordinary people to pursue a happy life.

During our conversation, he was asked to start with an introduction to his school.

The school for blind children in Lhasa now has 29 students. Since its establishment in 1997, it has helped more than 300 blind students to learn Braille, get to know and accept themselves and embrace society. The students are generally aged between 6 and 15. Like other students at general schools, they also need to learn English, Chinese Language, Tibetan Language and mathematics. After studying at the school for three years, they may choose to study from Grade Four in general schools like intact children. Since they have already learned basic Braille, it is relatively easy for them to study at general schools. Any general school that has teaching materials in Braille can satisfy their learning needs. What makes the school proud is that its students can go to school with intact students. They are admitted into lower secondary schools and upper secondary schools and even colleges.

During the conversation, he frequently mentioned the term "special education". He believed that special education is applicable to everyone instead of being specific to disabled people. People with disabilities have special learning needs, while intact people have theirs. He said very seriously, "Although you are doing special education research, I know more about blind people than you do. I know what they need best because I am blind myself".

He said in his TV interview, "As far as I am concerned, as blind people we must accept ourselves, that is, we must realize and acknowledge the fact that we are blind. Being blind is something that we cannot change, but it is entirely up to ourselves to be a good person or not. Our students are still young, and it is easy for them to learn knowledge. What I expect most from them is that they will become good people when they come into society. I think there are also good and bad blind people. The difference between people who can see and those who can't is that – let me give an example – if a blind person wants to borrow 200 Yuan from you, you may give the money to him immediately because he could take advantage of his blindness to win your trust easily. I think this is wrong. Blind people may also lie. Therefore, I hope that they can become good people in society in spite of their abnormality. In that case, people lend money to you not because you are blind but because they trust you. And they will treat you equally".

"Some people are rich, while others are poor. Some people have difficulty in learning knowledge, while others have physical defects. But all of us need a happy life. That's the same for us; we are just different in the way we pursue happiness", he added.

These words well explain his understanding of special education: everyone has special learning needs, and everyone is born equal. What is important is that we should recognize our uniqueness, face the unchangeable reality and try to be a good person.

Now he is famous, but he was once discriminated against because of his visual impairment. When he first became the principal, many people doubted that a blind person could be a good leader. He confessed that he had the same doubts, because sometimes, as a blind person, he was indeed powerless. However, he still had the courage to assume this responsibility. He told himself that there was nothing worse than his blindness, but he had overcome this serious difficulty and faced it boldly, so he would fear nothing else. With this in mind, he has done a brilliant job as a principal for blind children over the past few years.

He said that he did not work so hard, study so diligently and participate in various social activities so actively for his own fame or fortune. His real intention was to allow more people to learn about the lives and ideas of blind people and to make blind people better understood in the community. He explained,

> If we are not understood or accepted in the community, it is our own fault because we do not stand up. Nobody knows what kind of help we need and what we can do. That's why I hope all the blind people can get involved in the community and raise their voices. It is very important for them to do what they can in the community.

He thought that blind people should make friends with intact people and they may happily go out to eat with normal-sighted people. He himself has many friends with normal sight. "When we first become friends, they are worried about me in every particular and they think about what they can do to help me. But as we become familiar, they treat me as a member of their family".

He shared two anecdotes from his life that can lead to better understanding of how he got along naturally with his intact friends. He said that he likes drinking coffee very much. He would drink coffee with his friends as long as he is free. At first, his friends did everything they could for him, for example putting sugar into his coffee. Even though he could do it himself with ease, his friends were still worried and did it for him. "They were probably afraid that I might pour the sugar out of the cup", he laughed. However, after two or three meetings for coffee, his friends never did that for him again, because they knew that he could do it himself. Also, when he went to the bathroom, his friends immediately ran to turn on the light for him. He said his friends were worried that he could not see the switch, but they forgot that the light was useless to him. But after a long time, they naturally stopped doing that for him.

Happy smiles appeared on his face when he told these stories. It seems that he is satisfied with his life now, which he also said on TV. "I think happiness is a simple thing. You feel happy when you are contented and feel satisfied with your life. If you are not satisfied with your life, you won't be happy. If you feel contented, any small thing you do will make you happy".

When talking about the current education in the Tibetan regions, he thought that the existing education could not meet the students' needs, such as the needs for moral upbringing, survival skills and the learning of Tibetan cultural knowledge. He indicated that what blind students need most now is learning materials, especially in Tibetan Braille. He also pointed out that receiving education in special schools is the one and only choice for disabled students, because it is the choice made by the government and the community not by the students themselves.

Summary

Although stories such as that of the principal are few and far between, we recognize from this case that special education in the Tibetan regions lags far behind that in mainland China. Disabled children have fewer opportunities to receive educational interventions and start to be educated very late. The special education intervention model is relatively limited. Special education schools are virtually the only channel. However, if special education interventions for disabled adolescents are regarded as the top priority in special education and are seriously implemented, it will be beneficial for further research and practice in special education interventions for school-age and even pre-school disabled children in the Tibetan regions. It will also promote the rapid development of special education for children in the Tibetan regions. From this case, we can also clearly understand that special education interventions for disabled adolescents in the Tibetan regions should focus on improving their self-confidence and self-esteem, creating a social environment that they can integrate into and adapt to and providing them with more options to satisfy their needs.

In Appendix D, there are two diaries that provide a comprehensive record of the processes, methods and content of the author's investigations in the special education schools in the Tibetan regions, as well as his thorough understanding of the current special education interventions for disabled adolescents in the Tibetan regions. In particular, the recorded discussions with the teachers and parents in the dairies fully reveal how schools, the community, the government and families support special education interventions in the Tibetan regions. In the Tibetan regions, the community tolerates children with disabilities to some extent, but their social value and social contributions are not fully accepted in comparison to those of intact children. Although the government has increased its economic support year by year, there is a lack of investment in training their social adaptability and their survival skills and in constructing a good living environment for them. The parents tend to spoil and overprotect their disabled children and have poor awareness of their ability to receive education. They fail to recognize the development potential of their children. Instead, they focus on the children's attitudes and behaviours rather than their cognitive development. They barely support their school education. Although school education is developing rapidly and efforts are being made to explore and innovate special education interventions for disabled adolescents in the Tibetan regions that are adapted to the Tibetan community and culture, support is needed from the community, the government and parents.

In short, education for disabled children and adolescents in the Tibetan regions relies on special education interventions in special education schools. The development of special education interventions should focus on local social conditions and cultural foundations and should win support from the government, the community and parents.

Discussion

Questionnaires, interviews and narration are the most important research methods in this research. The theory of four levels of culture is an important theoretical basis and analytical tool. In the descriptive analysis of the questionnaire results, the analysis of the descriptive statistics and demographic variation is carried out for students, parents, teachers and other respondents respectively, discussing their educational concepts. Interviews provide a deep understanding of the educational viewpoints and attitudes of students, parents and teachers in a semi-structured way. These investigation data and result analysis are an important basis on which to discuss the value orientation of education in the Tibetan regions at present. The individual case study and survey log indicate the current situation of education in the Tibetan regions, especially special education in the Tibetan regions, as well as the thoughts of students, parents and teachers regarding this current situation. They represent further important investigative material for discussing the educational viewpoints of students, parents and teachers in the Tibetan regions. In this section, using the results of the questionnaires, interviews and narrations, with the theory of the four levels of culture as the analytical tool, the educational concepts of students, parents and teachers and their ideas, viewpoints and attitudes concerning education are discussed. Additionally, the current value orientation of education in the Tibetan regions is in process of modification.

Educational concepts of students, parents and teachers and similarities and differences between their educational viewpoints

In response to relevant questions in the questionnaire about their educational concepts, the three groups of respondents – students, parents and teachers in the Tibetan regions – provide the same or different answers. Therefore, it is highly necessary to analyse and discuss the educational concepts of students, parents and teachers and the similarities and differences between their educational viewpoints.

(1) Different answers concerning educational concepts and viewpoints

On the basis of the results of the questionnaire, interviews and survey, the students, parents and teachers have different answers to some questions, or they have certain differences in their choices.

In the questionnaire results, according to the statistical results of the significance frequency question, the parents think that, in addition to education, interpersonal relationships are very important. Most of the students and teachers agree with such a viewpoint. However, the students do not consider it very important in the same way as the parents. According to the statistical mean value and median results, the teachers think that acquiring knowledge and ability is more important than acquiring a diploma; however, the parents and students are not very sure about this. The students and teachers think an educated person may fail to find a job; like an uneducated person, an educated person also worries about not finding a job. However, the parents state that they are not sure about it, as they believe that receiving an education means getting a good job.

The interviews show that many of the parents do not know the studies of the students very well; they cannot judge whether the knowledge obtained by their children is expected by them and is required. The students who were interviewed think that the knowledge they are learning will be useful in their studies and life in the future. Most of the teachers who were interviewed think that the students learn knowledge according to the courses stipulated by the state, government and school, study in order to be admitted to a school at a higher level, and knowledge is not necessarily expected or required by them. Moreover, the students are unable to judge their own needs independently. This shows that the students, parents and teachers have different points of view when judging the value of educational content. All of the parents who were interviewed stated that they are satisfied with the current school education. A few of the students who were interviewed stated that they are not very satisfied with it; 50% of the teachers who were interviewed stated that they are not satisfied with the school education. This shows that the students', parents' and teachers' degree of satisfaction with the school education is different.

In the survey, we learned that the parents in the Tibetan regions pay more attention to the change in students' behaviour, and they do not pay much attention to the acquisition of knowledge, especially in special education schools. However, the students and especially teachers pay close attention to the acquisition of knowledge and they pay more attention to the results of examinations.

All the aforementioned conditions show that students, parents and teachers have their own points of view on education. However, as the differences tend to be a matter of degree, it is difficult to establish a significant difference in their viewpoints. All of them hold consistent viewpoints in terms of their educational concepts.

(2) Similar answers concerning educational concepts and viewpoints

According to the statistical results of the questionnaire in Appendix C, in the answers of the three different types of respondents, namely students, parents and teachers, to the 20 core questions, most questions show that there is a significant difference between different types of respondents. However, according to the statistical results for the mean value and median of the questions, the answers they select to these questions tend to be similar. In other words, their answers to these questions tend to be consistent. In response to the statement "higher education = good job security", according to the analysis of the variance of different types of respondents, P is less than the significance coefficient, namely Sig < 0.05. It shows that with regard to this question, a significant difference exists in the viewpoints of the different types of respondents. The mean value for this question of the three types of respondents is less than 3, and the median is 2.00. This shows that for the three types of respondents, the number of people who "agree" is higher than that of those who "disagree" with the statement. In other words, the answers the different types of respondents select for this question are consistent. Besides, according to the statistical results of significance frequency, most of the questions selected with relatively high frequency by the different types of respondents are the same. All these results show that the educational concepts of the students, parents and teachers and their educational viewpoints are basically consistent. In addition, in the interviews and narrative research, common ground between them as regards their concepts of education and educational viewpoints may be discovered.

To be specific, their common view of education is as follows: education is an important guarantee of personal achievement, occupational development and social recognition; education enables mankind to escape from poverty, and the educational level decides the income level and personal business start-up ability; education is not a waste of time, and everyone should receive an education and may study abroad to gain a better education; education has a function with regard to cultural inheritance and the promotion of the ideological and moral accomplishment of an individual, and the study and understanding of Tibetan historical culture and all-round development of the morality, intelligence, physique and aesthetics of humanity cannot be achieved without education.

The aforementioned thoughts about education and viewpoints on it include the assessment and value of education for the respondents' future financial well-being and the role of education in occupational development, educational quality, educational value and other aspects; they are important bases of the value orientation of education in the Tibetan regions.

The educational concepts of students, parents and teachers as value orientation of education in the Tibetan regions at present

The value orientation of education is the pursuit of or yearning for educational value and the selection of one or several schemes to meet one's own educational needs. The value orientation of education in the Tibetan regions refers to the students', parents' and teachers' pursuit of or yearning for educational value and educational schemes for the people in the Tibetan regions to meet their educational needs. Specifically, it is the students', parents' and teachers' educational concept and their common ideas about education, including the values and standard of value presented in their educational judgement, educational selection, educational implementation and educational evaluation to meet their needs.

According to the aforementioned discussion, the main contents of the value orientation of education in the Tibetan regions may be summarized as follows:

(1) Education is an activity involving the transmission of knowledge and the training of abilities. Teaching knowledge and cultivating human abilities are basic values of educational activities. Such a way of thinking is fully embodied in the results of the educational survey mentioned earlier in the Tibetan regions. However, in the specific practice of educational activities, what knowledge is taught and what skills are cultivated in school education in the Tibetan regions should be determined. Because of the unique natural living environment in the Tibetan regions and the history of civilization that goes back several thousand years, a lot of cultural knowledge and living skills adapted to the local society has been accumulated. At present, in the uniform nationwide educational evaluation, the screening of such knowledge and abilities has left certain negative effects.

(2) Education is an important approach to improving the quality of human life. Life is the most fundamental requirement of humans. Vulgarly, life means "survival". The quality of life expresses how to lead a better life based on "survival". In the Tibetan society, how to lead a better life may be understood as to how to lead a happy life. A happy life includes material needs and spiritual pursuits. The most fundamental material condition is a good income and a relatively good economic foundation. In other words, education can create a certain economic value. Additionally, an ideal occupation exists, and people can engage in their favourite jobs. In other words, education should embody the corresponding occupational value. Educational quality should be constantly promoted so that people could enjoy better education. The spiritual pursuit means respect for humans' beliefs and spiritual support. Therefore, another important value of education is bringing up humans to enjoy a happy life.

(3) Education is a lifelong process of promoting wisdom in humans and endowing humans with the dignity they deserve. For the core of Tibetan culture, it is the mercy and goodness of human beings, emphasized by their beliefs. Education aims to bring out the goodness in human beings. However, goodness is not unconditional and baseline-free, as it is established on the basis of wisdom. Only those who are good and wise can respect all living beings and truly realize that all sentient beings are equal. Only under such circumstances can all living beings be endowed with the dignity they deserve. In terms of such a way of thinking and its significance, the most fundamental purpose of education lies in promoting the wisdom of humans.

To sum up, education should meet the needs of the study of knowledge and the enhancement of abilities, improvement of the quality of life and the promotion of wisdom and acquisition of the dignity of the Tibetan people. Therefore, special education interventions aimed at disabled adolescents must inevitably be based on such educational value requirements and standards.

Limitations of this research

It is difficult to conduct field investigation in the Tibetan regions, especially at schools. If one does not have the relevant certificate from the local government and the competent department or one does not have friends at a school, one cannot enter the school, let alone conduct questionnaire and interview investigations. In this research, by making use of different relationships, the author was easily able to enter schools in the Tibetan region in order to conduct the investigation. As the researcher is Tibetan, once the researcher entered the school, he was able to communicate comfortably with the teachers and students. Besides, the researcher was easily able to win their trust. Such trust is very important, at least to the authenticity of the survey results. However, in the collection of some data, such as the number of disabled adolescents in the Tibetan regions, the number of different types of disabled adolescents, the basic distribution of disabled adolescents and other essential data, there are considerable difficulties. First, the government department does not have accurate statistical data regarding these aspects. Even if the government department had such data, it would be unwilling to provide it to the researcher. For a long time, this has been the most difficult-to-break research limitation for researchers on relevant problems in the Tibetan regions. Second, we tried to obtain essential data by collecting statistics in the field. However, as the Tibetan region is scantily populated and transport and other infrastructure conditions of the remote farming and pasturing areas are poor, no individual researcher is able to fulfil such a task. Although the missing statistical data do not have significant effects on this research, it is raised as a matter of difficulty.

6

CLOSING THE EXCURSION TO THE WORLD OF SPECIFIC VALUES

For the ultimate purpose of this research, by means of getting to know the educational concept of students, parents and teachers in the Tibetan regions, the current value orientation of education in the Tibetan regions has been identified, and special education interventions aimed at disabled adolescents within the context of such a value orientation have been discussed.

With value theory, intervention theory and the theory of four levels of culture as the theoretical basis and method for the research, a considerable amount of literature was collected to understand the traditional Tibetan culture. The research was conducted by the mixed method of a combination of quantitative and qualitative research. About 600 students of general secondary schools and special education schools, about 200 parents and about 200 teachers in the TAR, Tibetan region of Sichuan Province, Tibetan region of Qinghai Province and Tibetan region of Gansu Province were recruited for a questionnaire survey. Seven students, seven parents, seven teachers and four monks participated in semi-structured in-depth interviews. An in-depth investigation was conducted at five special education schools in the Tibetan regions.

From the questionnaire survey, the educational concept and educational viewpoint of the respondents can be ascertained. From the interviews, the degree of thought and understanding of the interviewees about education in the Tibetan regions at present can be ascertained. From the narration of the educational investigation, the current situation of education in the Tibetan region is ascertained. According to the aforementioned results and discussion, the following conclusions may be reached.

(1) The Tibetan nationality has a long history, a unique natural living environment and excellent traditional culture going back to several thousand years. Tibetan people believe in Buddhism, uphold wisdom, are merciful, pursue the cause of benefiting all sentient beings and think that all living beings are equal. Meanwhile, Tibetan people attach great importance to wisdom and the educational needs of life. However, school education aims gradually to increase the enrolment rate and pays

DOI: 10.4324/9781003268208-6

close attention to the acquisition of a diploma and a job. Interpersonal relationships play an increasingly important role in social life. Hence, the value orientation of education in the Tibetan regions is affected by the people's traditional culture and actual social conditions.

(2) Based on the common perception of people of different genders, different ages and different areas of educational needs, the value orientation of education in the Tibetan regions is a very current topic. It comprises the educational concept of students, parents and teachers and the similarity in their thoughts about education and viewpoints on it. A relatively stable need for a social group may also reflect the basic needs of different groups in the Tibetan regions for education at present. It shows that education can meet the needs of those who are being educated.

(3) Special education interventions in the Tibetan region are mainly reliant on education at special education schools. It is an important part of school education. However, the current value orientation of education in the Tibetan regions reflects the need for, the concept of and viewpoint on school education. Therefore, the value orientation of education in the Tibetan regions is the fundamental basis for special education interventions aimed at disabled adolescents.

(4) In the theory of four levels of culture, belief, as the cultural core layer, is the basis of the people's behaviour enabling them to meet their spiritual and material needs. According to psychology, a need is "a deficiency or unbalanced state in the organism. It embodies the reliance of the survival and development of the organism on objective conditions and it is the source of the organism's enthusiasm for activity" (Lin, Yang, & Huang, 2004, p. 1473). In terms of real society, disabled people lack respect for their equality in life. Therefore, the special education interventions aimed at disabled adolescents in the Tibetan region build their self-confidence and self-esteem. It is a process that enables them to gain the identity and dignity they deserve, which meets the outlook on life enshrined in Tibetan people's belief that "all sentient beings are equal". Besides, the interventions meet the disabled adolescents' need for personal equality and dignity.

(5) The parents of disabled children in the Tibetan regions pay special attention to whether education can bring two changes to their children. One is whether the attitude of the children changes, namely whether the children receive a good ideological and moral education and become kind-hearted and sensible people. The other is whether the children gain the ability to live independently through school education. Therefore, the ability to care for oneself is the goal and content of special education interventions aimed at disabled adolescents in the Tibetan regions.

(6) In the Tibetan regions, the traditional culture is deficient in terms of a tradition of school education, but it inevitably influences the life of the local people. Education should take into consideration the inheritance

> of ethnic culture and meet the basic needs for people's real social life. Therefore, special education interventions based on the cultural foundation and real social conditions of the ethnic group are optimal for disabled adolescents in the Tibetan regions. Special education interventions cannot be limited to the requirements of the inheritance of its traditional culture and adaption to the cultural values of the ethnic group. Moreover, they cannot only adapt to the real social requirements.

In short, based on the value orientation of education, educational interventions aimed at disabled adolescents in the Tibetan regions and provided mainly at special education schools respect the Tibetan traditional culture and the requirements of the society in the Tibetan region. The goals of special education interventions are "disabled adolescents gaining the dignity of everyone being equal" and "promoting the ability to care for oneself"; also, knowledge and abilities that meet the social needs in the Tibetan region and the disabled adolescents' own needs are taught, including the traditional Tibetan cultural knowledge and craftsmanship.

ANNEXURE

Questionnaires

Questionnaire 1: for students

A. I am: 1. Male __1___ 2. Female ___2___
B. My age
C. School: secondary education vocational education

Dear student, we would like to ask you to participate in research that is focused on your views on education. The questionnaire is anonymous. Please fill in all the items in the table. Circle the most valid answer.

Thank you for your time.

Please circle the response which best applies to you.

SA Strongly Agree	A Agree	DK Do not know	D Disagree	SD Strongly disagree

Q1	Higher Education = good job security.	**SA A DK D SD**
Q2	Education is the path to success at work.	**SA A DK D SD**
Q3	Education protects humans against poverty.	**SA A DK D SD**
Q4	Education is increasingly a guarantee of a higher income.	**SA A DK D SD**
Q5	Education encourages entrepreneurial activity.	**SA A DK D SD**
Q6	Highly educated people make up the nation's elite.	**SA A DK D SD**
Q7	It is worthwhile to go abroad for good education.	**SA A DK D SD**

(*Continued*)

Q8	Schools are not required.	**SA A DK D SD**
Q9	The main thing is a diploma.	**SA A DK D SD**
Q10	Contacts are important.	**SA A DK D SD**
Q11	Education in my country is a waste of time.	**SA A DK D SD**
Q12	Being able to work is the most important thing.	**SA A DK D SD**
Q13	One may make a good living without education.	**SA A DK D SD**
Q14	Most people should have an education.	**SA A DK D SD**
Q15	You cannot build a career without education.	**SA A DK D SD**
Q16	Professionalism is more important than education.	**SA A DK D SD**
Q17	Work will show up.	**SA A DK D SD**
Q18	Education can be afforded only by those who have the money for it.	**SA A DK D SD**
Q19	Graduation is required.	**SA A DK D SD**
Q20	An educated person need not worry about not finding work.	**SA A DK D SD**

Q21 The biggest influence on my ideas about education is my family. Yes □ No □

Q22 The biggest influence on my ideas about education is the school. Yes □ No □

Q23 The biggest influence on my ideas about education is my friends. Yes □ No □

Q24 The biggest influence on my ideas about education is the media. Yes □ No □

Questionnaire 2: for parents

A. I am the parent of: 1. a boy □ 2. a girl □ Age:

B. I am the father of the child the mother of the child My age Number of children in the family

C. My education is: junior high school secondary education vocational education university

Dear parent, we would like to ask you to participate in research that is focused on your views on education. The questionnaire is anonymous. Please fill in all the items in the table. Circle the most valid answer which is true for you in relation to your child. Thank you for your time.

Please circle the response which best applies to you.

SA Strongly Agree	A Agree	DK Do not know	D Disagree	SD Strongly disagree

Q1	Higher Education = good job security.	SA A DK D SD
Q2	Education is the path to success at work.	SA A DK D SD
Q3	Education protects humans against poverty.	SA A DK D SD
Q4	Education is increasingly a guarantee of a higher income.	SA A DK D SD
Q5	Education encourages entrepreneurial activity.	SA A DK D SD
Q6	Highly educated people make up the nation's elite.	SA A DK D SD
Q7	It is worthwhile to go abroad for good education.	SA A DK D SD
Q8	Schools are not required.	SA A DK D SD
Q9	Main's diploma.	SA A DK D SD
Q10	Contacts are important.	SA A DK D SD
Q11	Education in my country is a waste of time.	SA A DK D SD
Q12	Being able to work is the most important thing.	SA A DK D SD
Q13	One may make a good living without education.	SA A DK D SD
Q14	Most people should have an education.	SA A DK D SD
Q15	You cannot build a career without education.	SA A DK D SD
Q16	Professionalism is more important than education.	SA A DK D SD
Q17	Work will show up.	SA A DK D SD
Q18	Education can be afforded only by those who have the money for it.	SA A DK D SD
Q19	Graduation is required.	SA A DK D SD
Q20	An educated person need not worry about not finding work.	SA A DK D SD
Q21	I am satisfied with my child's education.	SA A DK D SD
Q22	I think the value of education is currently increasing.	SA A DK D SD
Q23	I wish my child to gain an education.	SA A DK D SD

Questionnaire 3: for teachers

A. I am: □ 1.Boy □ 2. Girl Age:

B. My education is: secondary education vocational education University □

Dear teacher, we would like to ask you to participate in research that is focused on your views on education. The questionnaire is anonymous. Please fill in all the items in the table. Circle the valid answer which is true for your statement. Thank you for your time.

Please circle the response which best applies to you.

SA	A	DK	D	SD
Strongly Agree	Agree	Do not know	Disagree	Strongly disagree

Q1	Higher Education = good job security.	SA A DK D SD
Q2	Education is the path to success at work.	SA A DK D SD
Q3	Education protects humans against poverty.	SA A DK D SD
Q4	Education is increasingly a guarantee of a higher income.	SA A DK D SD
Q5	Education encourages entrepreneurial activity.	SA A DK D SD
Q6	Highly educated people make up the nation's elite.	SA A DK D SD
Q7	It is worthwhile to go abroad for good education.	SA A DK D SD
Q8	Schools are not required.	SA A DK D SD
Q9	Main's diploma.	SA A DK D SD
Q10	Contacts are important.	SA A DK D SD
Q11	Education in my country is a waste of time.	SA A DK D SD
Q12	Being able to work is the most important thing.	SA A DK D SD
Q13	One may make a good living without education.	SA A DK D SD
Q14	Most people should have an education.	SA A DK D SD
Q15	You cannot build a career without education.	SA A DK D SD
Q16	Professionalism is more important than education.	SA A DK D SD
Q17	Work will show up.	SA A DK D SD
Q18	Education can be afforded only by those who have the money for it.	SA A DK D SD
Q19	Graduation is required.	SA A DK D SD
Q20	An educated person need not worry about not finding work.	SA A DK D SD
Q21	I think the value of education is currently increasing.	SA A DK D SD
Q22	I think the knowledge and skills students are learning are what they need and expect.	SA A DK D SD
Q23	I think that the knowledge acquired by students at school will have a major impact on their future studies.	SA A DK D SD
Q24	I think that the knowledge acquired by students at school will have a major impact on their future life.	SA A DK D SD
Q25	I am satisfied with students' education.	SA A DK D SD

Interview outline

For students

1 What subjects do you learn at school?
2 Do you study the Tibetan language at school?
3 What is your favourite subject? Why?
4 What is the subject you hate most? Why?
5 What is your daily schedule? (Please provide your daily schedule at school and during the weekend or holidays.)
6 Do you think what you are learning now will benefit your future studies? Why?
7 Do you think what you are learning now will be helpful in your future life? Why?
8 What do you most want to learn at school? Why?
9 Do you think it is necessary to learn the Tibetan language? Why?
10 Are you happy at school? Why?

For parents

1 Do you know what subjects your child learns at school?
2 What is your child's favourite subject? Why?
3 Does your child learn the Tibetan language at school?
4 Are you willing to send your child to school? Why?
5 Do you think children need to learn the Tibetan language at school? Why?
6 What do you think the children need to learn most at school? Why?
7 Are you satisfied with the school education? Why?

For teachers

1 Do you think the students are learning the knowledge and skills they need? Why?
2 Do you think the students are learning the knowledge and skills that they expect? Why?
3 Do you think the students need to learn the Tibetan language? Why?
4 Do you think what the students learn at school will greatly influence their future studies? Why?
5 Do you think what the students learn at school will greatly influence their future life? Why?
6 Are you satisfied with the school education? Why?

For monks

1 Can you briefly describe what you mostly learn?
2 What is your daily schedule?

3 What is the biggest change in you after receiving a temple education? Why?
4 What do you think is the biggest advantage of a monastic education? Why?
5 What do you think is the biggest shortcoming of a monastic education? Why?
6 What do you think about school education? Why do you think that?

The results of the ANOVA of different types of questionnaires

The results of the ANOVA of different types of questionnaires

		Sum of Squares	*df*	*Mean Square*	*F*	*Sig.*
Higher Education = good job security.	Between Groups	39.549	2	19.774	16.465	0.000
	Within Groups	1310.279	1091	1.201		
	Total	1349.828	1093			
Education is the path to success at work.	Between Groups	15.729	2	7.865	10.399	0.000
	Within Groups	822.091	1087	.756		
	Total	837.820	1089			
Education protects humans against poverty.	Between Groups	30.117	2	15.059	14.060	0.000
	Within Groups	1167.453	1090	1.071		
	Total	1197.570	1092			
Education is increasingly a guarantee of a higher income.	Between Groups	6.058	2	3.029	2.583	0.076
	Within Groups	1276.939	1089	1.173		
	Total	1282.996	1091			
Education encourages entrepreneurial activity.	Between Groups	17.621	2	8.811	11.098	0.000
	Within Groups	860.611	1084	.794		
	Total	878.232	1086			
Highly educated people make up the nation's elite.	Between Groups	13.843	2	6.921	6.440	0.002
	Within Groups	1168.349	1087	1.075		
	Total	1182.192	1089			
It is worthwhile to go abroad for a good education.	Between Groups	2.351	2	1.176	0.915	0.401
	Within Groups	1398.556	1088	1.285		
	Total	1400.907	1090			
Schools are not required.	Between Groups	2.366	2	1.183	0.878	0.416
	Within Groups	1463.801	1086	1.348		
	Total	1466.167	1088			
The main thing is a diploma.	Between Groups	23.360	2	11.680	11.039	0.000
	Within Groups	1149.070	1086	1.058		
	Total	1172.430	1088			

REFERENCES

Anderson, G., & Arsenault, N. (2005). *Fundamentals of educational research*. Philadelphia, Pennsylvania, USA: Taylor & Francis e-Library.

Bambara, L. M., & Knoster, T. P. (2009). *Designing positive behavior support plans*. Washington, DC: American Association on Intellectual and Developmental Disabilities.

Bandura, A. (1971). *Social learning theory*. New York: General Learning Press.

Chen, J. (2008). Ecological system model and revelation of early childhood intervention in European countries. *Journal of Modern Special Education* (4), 41–43.

Chen, Q. M. (2011). Analysis of the current situation and problems of special education in Tibetan Sichuan. *Journal of Sichuan University for Nationalities* (5), 96.

Chen, X. M. (2013). Thoughts on parents' participation in early interventions aimed at children with special needs. *Journal of Suihua University* (1), 146–149.

Dai, G. Y. (2011). Research on teacher training of special education in West China. *Chinese Journal of Special Education (Monthly)* (11), 66.

Dai, H. (2007). A study of the present situation and development strategies of special education in Tibet. *Journal of Research on Education for Ethnic Minorities* (3), 126.

De Lamarck, J. B. P. A. de M. (2011). *Philosophie zoologique: Ou, exposition des considérations relatives à L'Histoire naturelle des animaux* (vol. 1, 2). Cambridge, MA: Cambridge University Press. https://doi.org/10.1017/CBO9781139103817.

Deng, M. (2001). *The basic literature of foreign special education*. Beijing: Beijing University Press.

Deng, M., & Yan, T. R. (2016). Review on new progress of special education research in Western Countries. *Education Research* (1), 77–84.

Denzin, N. K., & Lincoln, Y. S. (1994). *Handbook of qualitative research*. Thousand Oaks, CA: Sage Publications.

Fairbanks, S., Sugai, G., Guardino, D., & Lathrop, M. (2007). Response to intervention: Examining classroom behavior support in second grade. *Exceptional Children*, *73*(3), 288–310. https://doi.org/10.1177/001440290707300302.

Ge, C. (2014). *A comparative study of deaf identity in Chinese Han, Tibetan Regions and Czech Republic* (Doctoral dissertation). Olomouc, Czech Republic: Palacky University.

Hofstede, G. (2001). *Culture's consequences: Comparing values, behaviors, institutions, and organizations across nations*. Thousand Oaks, CA: Sage Publications.

Holmes, M. S. (2004). *Fictions of affliction: Physical disability in Victorian culture*. Ann Arbor, MI: University of Michigan Press.
Huang, C., Li, X., Su, L., & Yang, Z. (2000). The effect of early intervention on toddlers' development. *Chinese Mental Health Journal*, *14*(1), 48–50.
Huang, S. M., Zhang, X. F., et al. (2008). Decision making in language intervention for special children. *Chinese Scientific Journal of Hearing and Speech Rehabilitation* (5), 64–69.
Huang, X. Y., Zhang, R., et al. (2009). An investigation of the needs of families and developmental support of 71 autistic children. *Chinese Journal of Special Education Monthly* (11), 43–47.
Jia, C. J. (2011). American special education intervention model. *A Journal of Modern Special Education* (1), 43–44.
Lei, J. H. (2008). *Preschool education for special children*. Wuhan: Huazhong University Publishing House.
Li, D. S. (2004). *The value of life*. Beijing: China Social Publishing House.
Li, F. F., & Yang, L. (2015). Application of sand play in interventions aimed at children with special needs. *Journal of Suihua University* (7), 136–138.
Li, H., et al. (2013). A cognitive study of metaphor and metonymy of time in Tibetan gesture language. *Journal of Minzu University of China (Philosophy and Social Sciences Edition)* (6), 160–165.
Li, L., & Zhang, F. J. (2007). A case study on early interventions for a child with a hearing impairment. *Chinese Journal of Special Education (Monthly)* (8), 24–27.
Lin, C. D., Yang, Z. L., & Huang, X. T. (2004). *Dictionary of psychology*. Shanghai: Shanghai Publishing House.
Ling, G., & Potměšil, M. (2017). A bibliometric analysis of current research situation of early intervention for exceptional children in mainland China. *Paidagogos*, *1*(8), 117–131.
Lipsky, D. K., & Gartner, A. (1998). Taking inclusion in to the future. *Educational Leadership*, *56*(2).
Liu, H. (2010). The autistic child: Behavioral intervention in rehabilitation status and suggestions. *Journal of Nanjing Technical College of Special Education* (3), 34–37.
Liu, L. Y., Mo, S. L., et al. (2014). On the deficits in facial expression recognition in children with ASD and clinical intervention. *Chinese Journal of Special Education* (2), 41–48.
Liu, Q. Y., Zhang, F., et al. (2008). Decision making in auditory interventions for special children. *Chinese Scientific Journal of Hearing and Speech Rehabilitation* (3), 68–71.
Liu, S. L. (2010). Means of coping with hearing-impaired children in families and the family-centered early intervention. *Chinese Journal of Special Education (Monthly)* (1), 19–24.
Liu, Y. J. (2013). Discussion of construction of a model of personalized comprehensive intervention aimed at children with ADHD. *Journal of Chinese School Education* (8), 180.
Mao, Y. Y. (1990). *Early detection and early intervention of mentally retarded children*. Beijing: Science Publishing House.

Marczyk, G., DeMatteo, D., & Festinger, D. (2005). *Essentials of research design and methodology*. Hoboken, NJ: John Wiley & Sons, Inc.
Mei, Z. H. (2014). Analysis of the Tibetan special education teacher training situation. *Tibetan Education* (3), 46.
Metzler, I. (2006). *Disability in medieval Europe : thinking about physical impairment during the High Middle Ages*, c. 1100–1400. Abingdon, Oxon: Routledge.
Mu, Y. S., & Wang, G. Y. (1997). New horizon of value philosophy research of China. *Journal of Guizhou University* (2), 44–47.
Nima, Badeng, & Liu, C. (2016). *The theory of dignity – research on the reconstruction of culture and creation of a harmonious society in the disaster area after the Wenchuan Earthquake*. Chengdu: National Publishing House.
Piao, Y. X. (1996). *Special education dictionary*. Beijing: Huaxia Publishing House.
Potměšil, M., & Valenta, M. (2006). *Chapters on special education*. Olomouc, Czech Republic: Palacky University Press.
Prathap, G. (2013). The cost of instruction, the value of education. *Current Science*, *104*(12), 1605.
Qian, L. X. (2008). *Effective participation strategies of students with different learning needs in ordinary school*. Beijing: Education Science Publishing House.
Qiu, X. J., & Wang, L. X. (2010). Parental involvement in the early intervention of children with autism and the factors that affect parental involvement. *Chinese Journal of Special Education (Monthly)*, *118*(4), 37–41.
Ruan, Q. (2004). *Value philosophy*. Beijing: Party School of the CPC Central Committee Publishing House.
Růžičková, V. (2017). Early intervention as a determinant of quality of life of individual with visual impairment. *Problemy Edukacji, Rehabilitacji i Socjalizacji Osób Niepełnosprawnych*, *1/2017*(1), 71–82.
Schein, E. H. (2010). *Organizational culture and leadership*. Hoboken, NJ: John Wiley & Sons, Inc.
She, W. B. (2014a). Investigation and reflection of special education in Sichuan ethnic areas. *Journal of Ezhou University* (12), 79.
She, W. B. (2014b). Exploring and analysing the "three elements" model of vocational education of disabled students based on the observation of disabled students in Sichuan special education schools. *Adult Education* (3), 49.
Shen, R. H. (2014). Research on the relationship model of social adaptation social support, and life satisfaction of Tibetan children with a hearing loss. *Journal of Chongqing Normal University (Natural Science)* (2), 110.
Sun, J. Z. (2004). Conditions and countermeasures of Chinese rehabilitation of deaf children. *Chinese Journal of Special Education (Monthly)* (2), 17–20.
Suo, Q., & Sun, W. Z. (2008). The development of Tibetan sign language contributes barrier-free communication for the deaf in Tibetan. *Human Rights* (3), 57–58.
Thornberg, R., & Oğuz, E. (2016). Moral and citizenship educational goals in values education: A cross-cultural study of Swedish and Turkish student teachers' preferences. *Teaching and Teacher Education*, *55*, 110–121.
Vargas-Barón, E. V., Janson, U., & Mufel, N. (2009). *Early childhood intervention. Special education and inclusion: A focus on belarus*. http://unesdoc.unesco.org.
Wang, W. D. (2002). *Educational values in the process of modernization*. Beijing: China Social Sciences Publishing House.

Wang, Y. G. (2000). Exploration and analysis of the theory of early childhood intervention. *Chinese Journal of Special Education (Quarterly)* (4), 1–3.

Wang, Y. G., Jia, L., et al. (2016). Autistic infants joint attention: Development models and early interventions. *Chinese Journal of Special Education (Monthly)* (6), 59–64.

Wiersma, W., & Jurs, S. G. (2010). *Research methods in education – an introduction* (9th ed.). Beijing: Educational Science Publishing House.

Windelband, W. (1893). Geschichte der Philosophie. *Philosophical Review* 2 (1), 119.

Wu, C. Y., Mao, Y. L., & Huang, H. (2014). Survey on the development of special education schools in minority areas. *Journal of Sichuan University for Nationalities* (5), 85.

Xu, Y., & Chen, L. J. (1995). Case study on early intervention aimed at mentally handicapped children – Understanding graphics and hand-eye coordination training. *Journal of Research on Children with Special Needs and Teachers* (3), 14–17.

Yang, X. J. (2003). Review of research on early interventions in mainland China. *Chinese Journal of Special Education (Bimonthly)* (4), 63–68.

Yao, D. (2012). Discussion on early interventions aimed at children with special needs. *Journal of Quanzhou Teacher College* (3), 1–3.

Zan, F. (2016). *Inclusive education: Ideals and practices.* Shanghai: Huadong Normal University Publishing House.

Zhang, D. S. (1934). *Value philosophy.* Shanghai: Shanghai World Press.

Zhang, F. J., Jiang, Q. D., et al. (2007). An investigation of the current situations of community intervention aimed at people with disabilities in Shanghai. *Chinese Journal of Special Education (Monthly)* (7), 23–24.

Zhang, F. J., & Yang, F. Y. (2011). *Early interventions aimed at children with special needs.* Shanghai: East China Normal University Press.

Zhang, L. L., Liu, X. X., & Lin, Y. X. (2019). Teachers' perception of the response to intervention implementation feasibility in Chinese inclusive early childhood education. *International Journal of Developmental Disabilities*, *65*(5), 387–395.

Zhang, L. Y. (2016). A preliminary study on the legislative system construction of early education for special children. *Legal System and Society* (30), 44–45.

Zhao, F. J. (1991). *Chinese traditional philosophy value theory.* Xian: Shanxi People's Publishing House.

Zhao, X. C. (2014). Initial research on Tibetan sign language: Talking about the sign language work of ethnic minorities in China as well. *Tibetan Studies* (2), 100.

Zhong, J. H., Han, P., Gao, X., & He, C. (2011). On Tibetan-language braille and its abbreviations. *Chinese Journal of Special Education (Monthly)* (10), 49.

Zhou, G., & You, Z. Y. (2007). Early interventions aimed at autistic children – A three-way training system. *Chinese Journal of Special Education (Monthly)* (5), 56–51.

Zhou, J. (2017). *Questionnaire data analysis: Six analytical thoughts to crack SPSS.* Beijing: Publishing House of the Electronics Industry.

Zhou, Y. (2015). *Research on Tibetan teachers' attitude towards inclusive education* (Doctoral dissertation). Palacky University, Olomouc, Czech Republic.

Legislative resources

U. S. Department of Health and Human Services. (1998). Head Start Program performance standards and other regulations (Part 1305.6). Washington, DC: U.S. Government Printing Office.

Individuals with Disability Education Act Amendments of 1997 [IDEA]. (1997). Retrieved from https://www.congress.gov/105/plaws/publ17/PLAW-105publ17.pdf

1 The National People's Congress. (1990). *The law of the People's Republic of China on the protection of disabled persons*. http://www.scio.gov.cn/32344/32345/32347/33466/xgzc33472/Document/1449134/1449134.htm
2 The State Council of the People's Republic of China. (1994). *The regulations on the education of persons with disabilities*. http://www.moe.gov.cn/s78/A06/jcys_left/moe_709/s3330/201001/t20100128_82037.html
3 The National People's Congress. (2017). *Maternal and infant health law of the People's Republic of China*. http://www.gov.cn/b.anshi/2005-08/01/content_18943.htm
4 The State Council of the People's Republic of China. (2001). *Opinions on further promoting the reform and development of special education during the tenth five-year plan*. http://www.gov.cn/gongbao/content/2002/content_61549.htm
5 The State Council of the People's Republic of China. (2017). *Regulations on disability prevention and rehabilitation*. http://www.gov.cn/zhengce/zhengceku/2017-02/27/content_5171308.htm
6 The Central Committee of the Communist Party of China and the State Council. (1993). *Education reform and development programme of China*. http://www.moe.gov.cn/jyb_sjzl/moe_177/tnull_2484.html
7 The National People's Congress. (1995). *Education law of the People's Republic of China*. http://www.npc.gov.cn/wxzl/gongbao/1995-03/18/content_1481296.htm
8 The Ministry of Education. (1999). *Action plan for vitalization of education facing the 21st century*. http://www.moe.gov.cn/jyb_sjzl/moe_177/tnull_2487.html
9 The National People's Congress. (2006). *Amending chairman's order No. 38 of the 6th session, Law of the People's Republic of China on compulsory* education. http://www.gov.cn/ziliao/flfg/2006-06/30/content_323302.htm

INDEX

Page numbers in **bold** indicate a table on the corresponding page.

Made in the USA
Las Vegas, NV
30 October 2024

d1de4279-f942-4607-b539-822b88426ec1R01